The politics of primary education

Edited by
Cedric Cullingford

Open University Press
Buckingham • Philadelphia

Open University Press
Celtic Court
22 Ballmoor
Buckingham
MK18 1XW

and
1900 Frost Road, Suite 101
Bristol, PA 19007, USA

First Published 1997

A catalogue record of this book is available from the British Library

ISBN   0 335 19578 4 (pbk)   0 335 19579 2 (hbk)

Library of Congress Cataloging-in-Publication Data
The politics of primary education / Cedric Cullingford (ed.).
     p.   cm.
   Includes bibliographical references and index.
   ISBN 0-335-19578-4 (pbk.). — ISBN 0-335-19579-2 (hard)
   1. Education, Elementary—Great Britain.   2. Education, Elementary—Political aspects—Great Britain.   3. Education and state—Great Britain.   4. School management and organization—Great Britain.   I. Cullingford, Cedric.
LA633.P63   1997
372.941—dc21   96-52126
                                                                         CIP

Typeset by Type Study, Scarborough, North Yorkshire
Printed in Great Britain by St Edmundsbury Press, Ltd, Bury St Edmunds, Suffolk

In memory of Bill Percival

Contents

Preface

The significance of primary education has long been recognized by those who understand how it influences people and their subsequent careers. Despite this, primary education has rarely captured the commensurate political and media attention. This was certainly true when Bill Percival created the Centre for Primary Education (which in 1982 became the Primary Education Study Group). He felt that such a group was needed for the following reasons:

> to draw public attention to the needs of primary education; to encourage the widest debate on the issues of importance; to initiate enquiries and research; to press continually for the search for quality; and to serve as a central forum for teachers, advisers, administrators, parents, researchers and politicians.[1]

Since the beginning of 1983 the group has met twice a year for a period spanning at least the better part of two days, always with an inner core of 25 or so permanent members representing all the interests of primary education as well as those in positions to influence policy. To that permanent group has always been added invited guests, usually a few and occasionally, for larger conferences, the vast majority. These guests have tended to be class teachers; just those people, like parents, who Bill Percival felt were unrepresented.

It is typical of Bill Percival that he should not only have seen a need for such a group but also acted upon it. At the time he was principal of Charlotte Mason College, University of Lancaster, famous for the degree in

Applied Education focusing attention on the quality of primary class-rooms. He was an inspired and surprising choice as principal since his background was in secondary education, having been head of Bicester School, one of the largest comprehensives in Great Britain. In the quota-tion above we see a hint of some of the qualities of the man. He had a deep concern for education and wanted to draw public attention to its import-ance. At the same time he did not want to use propaganda; he felt that good intellectual debate should be disinterested rather than driven by political dogmas. He felt strongly about the qualities of the best teachers, but was no ephemeral encourager of the second rate. He cared passion-ately about quality, and was always eager to seek it out and nurture it. He was in the best sense a modest man, not just modest about his own achievements but quick to give recognition to those of others. He is much missed.

This book is not just dedicated to Bill Percival's memory but arises out of his work. All the contributors are or have been members of the Primary Education Study Group.[2] The aim of the book is to be worthy of him by being a work of quality and usefulness in itself. While the first chapter uses the Primary Education Study Group as a platform and an exemplar, its concern is with the political issues of primary education, both those that change and those that remain the same. Although we live in times when education has become a party-political issue as never before, and a subject of close involvement by politicans as never before, the politics that the book describes is concerned with those issues which make the most impact on teachers, children and parents. The list of chapters encapsulates points of controversy and debate that are not ephemeral but remain at the heart of a concern for primary education.

Bill Percival would have wanted the book to be based on research and expressed as lucidly and interestingly as possible. He was all for the clear communication of evidence. Thus we have a series of chapters that analyse the realities of primary education, how it has changed, what forces have impinged upon it and what are the elements that remain constant over the years. These range from the most external, such as the impact of market forces on the control and development of primary schools, to the most inti-mate, such as children's actual experiences of primary schools. In between these two extremes lie all the issues that have an impact on teacher's lives, the curriculum and teaching styles, parents and assessment, governors and local authorities. What is clear in all the chapters is that the original concern for primary education, and the issues that are being discussed, is as important as ever. What has changed is that there is no longer a sense that primary education is being neglected. Whether that is a good thing remains a more ambiguous and difficult question than Bill Percival would have envisaged in 1982.

Note

1 S.W. Percival, 'The future of the Centre', paper presented to the Primary Education Study Group (December 1984).
2 In addition, I would like to acknowledge the help of Richard Howard.

List of contributors

Robin Alexander is Professor of Primary Education and Director of the Institute for Education at the University of Warwick. His many writings on primary education led him to be invited to be one of the 'three wise men'.

Neville Bennett is Professor of Primary Education at the University of Exeter and author of many research reports, including *The Quality of Pupil Learning Experiences*.

Tim Brighouse is now Director of Birmingham City Education Authority, having been Professor of Education at Keele University as well as a well-known public speaker and writer.

Cedric Cullingford is Professor of Education at the University of Huddersfield. Recent books include *The Effective Teacher*, *Children and Society* and *The Inner World of the School*.

Mary Jane Drummond is tutor in Primary Education at the University of Cambridge Institute of Education. Her recent books include *Assessment in Primary Schools*.

Dr Philip Hunter is Chief Education Officer for Staffordshire and an educational consultant.

Gillian Pugh is Chief Executive at the Thomas Coram Foundation and famous in particular for her work on the early years of pre-school and schooling.

Felicity Taylor is Director of the Institute of School and College Governors and represents governors' interests on the Primary Education Study Group.

Dr David Winkley is head of the Grove Primary School in Handsworth, Birmingham, and Director of the National Primary Centre.

1

Changes in primary education

Cedric Cullingford

British primary schools have long had a unique reputation. Visitors from overseas have come looking for the distinct signs which have long been associated with British primary schools and epitomized in the Plowden Report[1] on primary education: not the superficial symbols such as double-mounted wall displays or the attractive arrangements of natural materials such as the often-used collections of teasels, but the emphasis on children learning rather than being taught. Comparisons between the role of teachers in other countries and in Great Britain have shown how different they are.[2] Unlike their counterparts elsewhere, British primary teachers have taken on an extended role, feeling responsible for the emotional, social and moral welfare of their pupils and not just for the delivery of the curriculum. It is this role of teachers, more than anything else, that has given primary schools their distinctive ethos, and this is a perception of teachers that also has echoes in the recent debates about the National Curriculum.

The reputation of primary schools is, however, a double-edged sword. The openness and responsiveness of teachers towards children and their parents might have attracted attention from educators from all over the world, but it also attracted criticism. The Plowden Report was associated with a softness, an inefficiency of approach, and a consequent lowering of standards. The apologists for that approach did not always help by their very enthusiasm for the language of 'child-centred' and 'discovery learning'.[3] The problem was, and remains, the fact that reputations are not always based on a rational analysis of the facts but on mythologies, or images as ephemeral as wall displays. Any empirical look at primary schools over the last few years has shown that the actual practice is only rarely a parody or an extension of the Plowden reputation.[4] But this does not in any way diminish the dominance of anecdote over evidence.

Analysis of the teaching styles observed in primary schools shows how varied they are.[5] But one characteristic that has marked out the approach of teachers, whether developed as a philosophy or not, is the attention given to the concept of enablement – enabling children to learn. The awareness of this approach has gained both a reputation and the suspicion of politicians. What has changed, as a result, is that primary schools have attracted more political attention. All the concerns that the politicians have expressed since 1979 have been with the curriculum, from the 'core' curriculum to the National Curriculum. Their attention is on what they can control, what is 'delivered' and 'assessed', rather than on the 'secret gardens' of children's minds. This has profound, if subtle, implications for teachers. One can acknowledge the difference between myth and reality: for example, the fact that the 'core' curriculum – the 'basics' of maths, reading and writing – has dominated primary schools, for all the complaints of their absence. But at the heart of primary education is the role of the teacher: the relationship between personal autonomy and decision-making and the submission to outside control.[6]

If the reputation of primary schools has proved a double-edged sword, so has the interest of politicians. There was a time when primary schools seemed to be entirely ignored. When Bill Percival founded in 1981 what was then called the Centre for Primary Education (now the Primary Education Study Group) it was in response to this neglect. All attention in the early 1980s seemed to be on comprehensive reorganization and falling rolls. This reflected not so much the significant issues but the fact that the people who made important decisions represented the interests of secondary schools. Bill Percival, himself with a secondary background, recognized that there was a 'pressing need for the establishment of a credible and recognizable "voice" for primary education'.[7] It is worth noting, however, that far from being associated with the viewpoint of a narrow or prejudiced point of view this 'voice' was to be not only powerful but independent.

The gap between myth and reality has already been noted. It is significant that from the beginning those who, with Bill Percival, felt concerned about primary education held on to the belief that evidence rather than prejudice, the truth rather than political will, was important. The voice to which Percival referred had to 'speak from a platform which [would] give it credibility and continuity, one related to current practice in schools, to perceived problems and to relevant research'.[8] What was then felt to be lacking was disinterested concern for primary education, recognizing its importance rather than using it as a political toy. There was an essential seriousness in the concern: taking teachers seriously, stressing the need for communication and searching for real quality. While there was no complacency – a far cry from the view of self-indulgence held by some outsiders – the need was for philosophical neutrality rather than politically driven ideas, for a balance between research and practice rather than dogma and anecdote.

The emphasis in primary education has traditionally been on the role and skills of teachers. This is because they are responsible for such a variety of subjects, concepts and skills that outsiders often wonder how they manage. But such a pressure stresses the difficulties that teachers face. The Primary Survey of 1978 and the Oracle Report raised important issues about classroom priorities and organization. The recognition of the difficulties teachers faced and a celebration of their success when they overcame them was what informed and motivated the founders of the Primary Education Study Group in the early 1980s. But at the time primary education was still an area that had not attracted attention. Teachers had autonomy. They seemed to live in private spaces. The closest threat to them was the idea of open-plan schools, the intrusion of the outsider 'with enforced collaboration' into the personal and enclosed world of the teacher.[9]

Whatever happened within the confines of the schools, there was great concern on the outside. This was encapsulated in the almost symbolic failure of the William Tyndale School, a failure of accountability and control, just those factors that more recently have been of such high salience.[10] The William Tyndale School affair demonstrated the extremes of teachers going entirely their own way in the name of child-centredness without taking account of the wishes of parents – for example, that their children should learn to read and write. But the concern was not, as in the aftermath of that incident, focused only on blame, but on the need for high-level support for best practice. Those who represented the 'great and the good' in primary education agreed that

> there should be a high level group [focusing] its discussion and thinking on the sector of primary education with the object of influencing those who shape policy and ensuring that primary education is kept firmly on the national agenda.[11]

This 'group' was not to be a fixed 'centre' – of which there are many – but a representative collection of people who could give a voice to all those who are concerned with primary education, or at least a voice to all except the children. The group represented teachers, parents and governors, as well as chief education officers, journalists, the Department of Education and Science (DES), Her Majesty's Inspectorate (HMI) and academics. It always reconsidered its own membership.

A group discussing itself as well as primary education might be considered to be involved in a certain amount of navel-gazing. But membership raised two issues of fundamental importance which have been at the heart of primary schools for many years. The first is the question of gender. It is noticeable that those who spoke for, and speak for, primary education – for instance, the professors and the chief education officers – tend to be men. One might either find it significant or take it for granted that the study group founded to defend and speak for primary education, and particularly teachers in that sector, should be men. But that is only half the point.

The second issue of concern is the desire to attract practising classroom teachers to the group. There were and are difficulties in helping giving them a 'voice'. One was the question of enfranchising them. Lack of resources, and modesty, meant that those class teachers who came tended to be 'plucked out' of their obscurity. Another was the fact that soon after their accommodation into the group they would be promoted – to lectureships, to headships or to advisory posts. Mention has been made of the need to give a 'voice' to primary education, but to give a voice to the majority of the teachers in primary education was and is more problematic. While this is not the place to give even a short account of the relationship between the ethos of the primary school and the way in which it is viewed in society, the discussion of the role of teachers should be read bearing this significant point in mind.

Primary education has been politically marginalized not only because of the gender issue but also because it represents long-term investment. Anticipation rather than response, the long term rather than the short, evaluation rather than assessment are not commodities much favoured by politicians who think only of the next election. One of the reasons for the neglect of primary education, for all its importance, is the fact that its effect in social and economic terms is long-term. However explicit the empirical evidence, the results lie beyond the political life of those who make decisions. In Bill Percival's vision the group designed to speak for primary education was established 'with the object of influencing those who shape policy and ensuring that primary education is kept firmly on the national agenda'.[12] Given the marginalization of teachers, and the short-term thinking of politicians, the question was who were the most important body of people who could have an influence. In many respects the answer to that seemed to be the parents – those who were being spoken for by the government whether they liked it or not.

One of the most significant, if subtle, changes to primary education, and the role of teachers, has been the strengthening of the involvement of parents.[13] This involvement has been far more successful in terms of parental support, whether formal or informal, than in terms of parental control. The involvement of parents as ancillaries or as teachers of reading might remain more occasional than universally implemented, but it is the first tentative sign of a recognition of parents as having a role to play in the education system, a realization that the earliest years in children's lives are crucial in educational terms.[14]

When we look back on the debate about the involvement of parents we can see both the underlying political forces at work and the nature of the controversy. In 1987 Bill Percival wrote a short paper on primary education and parents.[15] Many of the subsequent arguments about accountability and control are foreshadowed in it.

> Parents are increasingly invoked in the bitter war of words raging through education on the issues of provision, accountability, and above all control. 'Invoked' conveys the right degree of insubstantiality, for though there are many promises and worthy aspirations very little real power has been [prised] away from those who traditionally hold it – the politicians, the officers (both DES and Town Hall varieties), the teachers' unions, the heads and the pundits.
>
> Where are those parents and how do we seek their views on major issues (such as the nature of the curriculum, discipline, values, exams, records, the shape of the school year), when they are on the national agenda? We have no recognised national body with a clear constituency and brief. Nor do we have any agreed understanding as to exactly what should be the role of parents and their relationship with the education service.
>
> Meanwhile, in spite of this blank conceptual map, action and promises abound. The 1986 Act takes away from the [local education authorities] the final responsibility for the curriculum and hands it to the governors but requires them in turn to report annually to parents. The Labour Party promises a charter of parents' rights. The previous Secretary of State tried (but failed) to give parents the controlling voice on governing bodies; cooperation between teachers and parents in assisting learning. Everything is flowing in the same direction and parents are clearly good news. How has it all happened?
>
> We have first to recognise that it isn't one movement, but rather the results of three quite distinct developments – parents as governors, parents as consumers and parents as educators.
>
> The first has been given stimulus by that side of the Government's thinking which aims to give power to the periphery and which seems to balance so oddly with the other aim of pulling greater power to the centre.
>
> The second force is that of an increasingly confident and articulate consumerism. In a world in which education and the media have encouraged the ideal of the critical consumer there is little reason for not applying the same approaches to the doctor, social worker, housing officer or teacher. The professional–lay relationship has radically changed, as much in Hackney as in Henley.

The third force is the only one which comes from education itself, the product of a creative response from teachers and advisers to important research. Based on the concept that parents are the first educators and hold the key to how effective others can be, it demonstrates how this key could be turned. For some time now schools as far apart as Strathclyde and Hackney, Rochdale and Coventry, have established partnership patterns of significance and import.

However, the effect of these forces, whether they will strengthen or harm the education service in its present delicate condition, remains in doubt.

Consumerism, the tensions between the centre and the periphery and the struggle between creative innovation and control are all clearly spelled out here.

While Bill Percival recognized in the 1980s the significance of parental involvement, he was still concerned with 'influencing those who shape policy and ensuring that primary education is kept firmly on the national agenda'.[16] With hindsight there is a certain irony in this statement. Close government interest in primary education has not necessarily proved a blessing. What the Primary Education Study Group wished to do, realizing early on that the government wished to change and control the education system, was to try to ensure that it would do so based on evidence, rather than on dogma. That is what gave urgency to the discussions. By 1984 representatives of the Department of Education and Science were saying that 'whether the Secretary of State could or should be involved in the curriculum was no longer worth debating. The nature of the involvement and the consequences for LEAs were now the issues'.[17] Much discussion took place about the distinction between a consensus on the curriculum in primary schools and a national syllabus. And much discussion ensued about how the Secretary of State would try to influence schools. The signs of the changes were there, but no one could have anticipated the extent of centralization and control.

Nevertheless, reflecting on all the discussions that took place over the years, one is struck not only by all the changes but also by the sense of familiarity. We witness both the prophetic, the anticipation of things to come and which are now familiar, and the sense that the real issues of primary education do not change. Whatever a government introduces there will be major themes of concern, such as the curriculum, the quality of educational achievement and the role of teachers. The sense of continuity in primary education is important. It is not a sign of complacency or the unexamined acceptance of established practice. On the contrary, it derives from concerns which are profound, and not mere passing whims. It is concentrated on what the pupils are learning rather than on the time spent on tasks, on the development of intellectual skills, aesthetic appreciation and moral understanding rather than on whether the teaching is 'formal' or 'informal'.

Discussions among teachers might include encouragement but they also enter into uncomfortable areas; they open up awareness at a variety of levels. One of the issues that dominated the meetings of the Primary Education Study Group over the last ten years was what constitutes the primary curriculum. The way this was approached was as a challenge, an attempt to think of the real educational issues. In Walter Ulrich's words:

> What needs to be tackled is the still far too prevalent tendency for primary schools to expect too little of their pupils, and so to fail to stretch them to their full potential, in all aspects of the curriculum ... One difficulty is that there is no broad consensus about what constitutes the primary curriculum ... We lack both a broad definition in terms of subject coverage and personal and social development.[18]

The driving issue that is seen to affect the curriculum is not only at the level of 'coverage' but also pupils' understanding – in terms of not only the measurable regurgitation of fact but also the more difficult and challenging effects on behaviour and action:

> We carry all too easily and subconsciously the attitudes and turns of phrase that come from an analysis of the curriculum based upon the timetable. The mental set is of functions separated by time and, among inspectors, by personal specialism ... We need a reformulation of the curriculum in a simple, even if deceptively simple and holistic way. The outcome of analysis should be synthesis.[19]

The arguments about the curriculum are always to do with the level at which it is to operate, and the tensions between the parts and the whole. There was a time when people talked of the 'transfer' of skills from one subject to another. This focused attention on the ability to think, to be critical or to engage in rational argument. Such skills are not easily measurable and have therefore tended to be ignored. Memory is important but only in the service of thought. The terminology might have changed but the concept is as important as ever.

The tensions which surround the organization of the curriculum also reverberate in the question of the role of teachers. Are they specialists or generalists, managers of learning or deliverers of all knowledge? For a number of years there have been attempts made to measure what it is that teachers do: but this has also led to limiting the definition to what is measurable. And then to whom and for what are teachers accountable? David Winkley and Richard Howard asked:

> How do we move to an increasingly close consensus of view as to what excellence in teaching is without closing our options or

strait-jacketing the diversity (and experimental potential) of practice? How do we press teachers towards increasing excellence of practice and make them seem publicly accountable – and sympathetic towards critical assessment – without reducing the job to imposed formulae with considerable limitations of teacher autonomy?[20]

Throughout these years of discussion the concern has been the improvement in quality in primary education through encouraging the best practice in teaching. This inevitably raises questions of political control. How can, for example, those teachers who could be better, be encouraged or forced to improve? This concern is dubbed 'political' not because of the imposition of dogmas, or manifestations of personal power and marketing, but because there are definite means to improving the ends, and the argument is always about the alternative strategies. While one side might seem to win the argument, or, if not actually win it, have the political muscle to match one point of view, the argument remains essentially the same. The ancient educational debate is always with us:

> The contrasts are none the less stark for being so familiar. On the one hand, children's needs and the value of first-hand experience; on the other, society's needs, national norms and the mastery of information. The 'how' of education as opposed to the 'what', process to product; means to ends; diversity to uniformity; and assessment as diagnosis to assessment as measurement or accounting, from curriculum as a seamless robe, the whole much more than the sum of its parts, to curriculum as a collection of core and foundation subjects, from curriculum negotiated within an agreed framework at school level, to curriculum centrally 'constructed' and 'delivered', postman-style, by the teacher.[21]

In a time of rapid and almost wilful change the essential verities remain. They informed and inform discussion about the actual realities of classrooms. While the debates about the curriculum and the role of the teacher tended to dominate they were carried on in a context which recognized the expectations and aspirations of parents. Issues such as the early years and pre-school education, the teaching of reading and accountability all invoke a wider clientele, the wider participation of a greater audience than those with direct political control. Thus the subjects that the Primary Education Study Group discussed kept raising matters that showed not only how every individual child in the primary school, as well as every teacher, needed to be taken into account, but that education was and is too important a matter to be confined to schools.

The subjects of the Primary Education Study Group conference and meetings were planned some six months ahead and included special education needs, management, urban education, quality, class size, reading and teacher education. The intention was to anticipate issues rather than follow trends, to influence policy rather than reflect it. In his paper on the significance of parents, Bill Percival pointed out that all changes depended on how they were perceived and handled by teachers. He concluded:

This open and constantly changing world will impose strains on teachers; many will not cope. It will require from them new insights and fresh skills, and the resilience to live with ambiguity, compromise and negotiation. They will need the support of an equally hard thinking, committed and resilient parent constituency. If we fail to get both we shall be in deep trouble.[22]

Schools are complex social systems that, despite the most frantic legislation, do not change overnight. Many of the changes that have been seen to have taken place do not really affect the central point of schools – the children. The people most affected by change, by the mass of legislation and the mountains of documentation, are the teachers themselves. The most significant shifts of emphasis are in the role of the primary school teachers, including the role of head from curriculum leader and colleague to financial controller and chief executive.

People who take a disinterested view of primary teachers, and who observe them at work in their schools, come to the conclusion that over the years they have become better trained, more professional and more skilled, as well as more approachable. In 1984 Bill Percival wrote of them thus: 'We are now building up a teaching force, not only competent in the classroom crafts but also equipped to think more deeply and independently about what they are doing and why'.[23] By that time all new teachers had four years of preparation for their profession, whether they came into it through the BEd or PGCE routes. The focus of their professional development was on the practical and theoretical issues that permeate primary schools. This concentration on professional issues has consistently been noted by parents as resulting in rising standards.[24] And yet teachers have seemed beleaguered by constant criticism by the government. When parents and others have tried to express their belief in the dedication and professionalism of the majority of teachers they have been brushed aside as either irrelevant or misguided. Why?

There are two reasons that one can pick out from the complexity of a highly political and anxious time. The first is the desire for political control. For many years what went on inside primary schools seemed mysterious, full of unknowns. Classrooms were viewed as secret places, in which teachers could indulge themselves and experiment. The constant attack on the myth of an 'educational establishment', which has socialist leanings, is a result of the sense of ignorance, and a desire to get a firm grip on what goes on.[25] The second is the dogmatic belief in the spirit of competition, a strong belief that the only motivation that can drive people on is to better themselves at the expense of others.[26] Thus secrecy was seen to be allied to complacency. All aspects of the reputation of primary schools – cooperation, the sharing of ideas, the encouragement of experimentation and the celebration of children's achievement – was inimical to the spirit of competition.

The consequences of this political will took time to manifest themselves in actions. Long before the introduction of measures to disfranchise teachers there were overt attacks on their competence and professionalism. The poor state of primary teachers' morale was observed by the Primary Education Study Group throughout the 1980s. Each reform became an incremental one in the changing of the role and status of teachers. First was the growing accountability to parents and to governors. This was followed by appraisal, then by the introduction of a centrally determined curriculum with its attendant battery of tests, and the financial accountability of schools. Then came the increased attention paid to inspection, more and more allied to the appraisal of individual teachers and the control of teaching styles. The basic shift of emphasis has been from endorsement to assessment, from support to criticism.

This change has been a gradual one, and while the legislation, the enforcement, has been comparatively recent, the signs were there much earlier. From the point of view of the primary teacher there have been fairly constant tensions in the definition of the role. One tension is the balance between the delivery of knowledge and the creation of the right conditions for learning. Another is the relationship between the specialist knowledge of a particular subject and the general ability to cover the whole range of the primary curriculum. The Bullock Report on language and literacy drew attention to the dichotomy between the specialist and the generalist in that every teacher was seen as a teacher of English at the same time that the subject demanded a specialist input.[27] The Inner London survey of 75 schools in 1984 called for more specialists offering a greater range of expertise, even suggesting that the ideal number of teachers in a school was ten so that they could cover all aspects of the curriculum, including assessment.[28] The underlying conclusion was that, however important the role of class teachers, they could not be expected to cover knowledge of every subject in depth. There was therefore a real dilemma. Children were assumed to be capable of pursuing various subjects to a high level. Were teachers properly equipped to help in all of them? This is still an unresolved problem.

The difficulties facing teachers are real. The expectations grow higher as the abilities of children become recognized. The support for teachers, both moral and in terms of resources, has been diminished. The question remains whether the best response to these difficulties would come from the schools themselves, or from some agency elsewhere. All international reports, based on many years of research, agree that the reform and improvement of education systems depend on a combination of both.[29] There might be central directives but these are towards incremental change. Without the close involvement of teachers, including their decisions and sense of ownership, these reforms come to nothing. In Great Britain, perhaps uniquely, there is a dislocation. If one lists all the conclusions of international surveys and reports, from the developed and the developing worlds, they are entirely consistent, and put into action virtually everywhere except in Great Britain. The concerns are real. The question is how they are met.

A good example of different responses to the demands of the curriculum is that of a school ten years ago, before the imposition of centralized control, and that of a school today. On the intentions and the stated aims there are clear consistencies. The question remains open as to how these are best met. A case study of an inner-city school with a strong representation of minority ethnic groups was presented to the Primary Education Study Group several years ago. Many of the comments point to both the similarities and the differences from the present time. Before the National Curriculum the school had to work out for itself what should be taught, and how and why. This implied a lot of negotiation among staff. The result was that the school had worked out a taxonomy of values in which the curriculum was there to answer individual needs. At the core was the ethical development of children and their inner lives, including their feelings, the attitudes of teachers and parents. Out of the recognition came the need to assess, with the focus consistently on individuals and the resulting actions provoking teachers into thinking about the relevance of their actions. Such an approach led to an agreed and heavily discussed curriculum, which included not only those subjects prescribed by the National Curriculum but also others. The crucial difference was the planning which meant that certain parts, such as maths, were highly structured while others could be open-ended. The whole timetable was based on four premises: that the curriculum was in the hands of the teachers themselves; that planning allowed for a great deal of flexibility; that teachers were committed to this way of working; and that it was open to constant revision and change.

This study was of a school which both recognized the dilemmas of the curriculum and was determined to respond to them. Its teachers had to define their aims and purposes, which meant both many meetings and the use of external advice. This approach to the curriculum was seen to have particular benefits: it provided variety for children; it made sense to children and teachers; its flexibility provided cross-fertilization; it led to end-products; it encouraged teachers to think and discuss; it did not depend on written documentation or prescribed forms; it was open to change; and it harmonized staff.

It can be argued that every curriculum in every school will be based on similar principles, but the question is whether such an energy, a determination to create a whole-school policy for its own sake, is the same as responding to the demands of external agencies embodied in assessment and inspection. The ideals do not change. There is a constant need to raise standards, to recognize and respond to the potential of each individual, and to do this through constant diagnosis with reference to a sense of purpose that the school is trying to promote. The question which remains unsearched is whether the best teachers or the best schools do have the freedom to develop high standards or whether such a personal sense of purpose is taken away from them.

The reputation of British primary schools lay in the assumption that they listened to children, and that it was the interests of children which came first. In the age of the Children Act there is an irony here. Bill Percival talked of giving primary education a 'voice'. But who now has a voice that is heard? Is attention paid to the needs of the children or to facts that are delivered to them? Are parents or teachers listened to? When the Primary Education Study Group was founded there was still a belief that if there was enough reason and evidence there would be those who would hear. But listening and learning are professional activities. Talking is a political one. We find ourselves in an age in which primary education has become highly political. A battle is being fought for control, which may prevent the teaching profession from holding on to its autonomy. Political control means operations that command market forces. The apparent power of governors over teachers and the power of inspectors over governors, and the use of 'hit squads' to take over schools, are but a sample of such control.

Of course, the everyday reality of schools is more complex than this. Schools are as varied as ever; indeed, if league tables and parental choice were to succeed, this variety would be more pronounced, producing ever greater contrasts between the successful and the unsuccessful. Children go on learning and teachers teaching, but the sense we are left with is that this is increasingly in spite of, not because of, outside interference. Those principles which operated in the case study are still the ones which primary teachers would recognize. They are very demanding to anyone wishing to do a good job, but they are worthwhile.

Nothing affects people as much as insecurity and anxiety. We live in an age where there seems to be almost a relish in such anxiety. This affects teachers, and through them, their pupils. Parents recognize this and are disturbed by it. Children appear to carry on regardless but are deeply affected by what they see on television, what they witness on the streets, and what they are warned against by their parents. Teachers talk more and more of pressure and of stress. Primary schools might have seemed to outsiders as warm, secret gardens of security in an otherwise difficult world. To have disturbed them might have appeared a necessary political decision. But primary schools were never as cosy as that to those who took them seriously. They did, at best, offer an access to, and means to contribute to, a better world.

Bill Percival was a man who had high standards. He did not approve of the second-rate. But he could recognize the virtues of teachers as well as the failures. He wanted to support and celebrate the best of what primary teachers could do. He wanted to make the best practice articulate and recognized. Such a voice should not be silenced.

Notes

1 Central Advisory Council for Education, *Children and Their Primary Schools* (London: HMSO, 1967).
2 See, for example, P. Broadfoot and M. Osborn, with M. Gilly and A. Paillet, 'Teachers' conceptions of their professional responsibility: some international comparisons', *Comparative Education*, 23(3), 287–302 (1987).
3 G. Blenkin and V. Kelly, *The Primary Curriculum* (London: Harper & Row, 1981).
4 Department of Education and Science, *Primary Education in England: A Survey by HM Inspectors of Schools* (London: HMSO, 1978); S.N. Bennett, C. Desforges, A. Cockburn and B. Wilkinson, *The Quality of Pupil Learning Experiences* (Hove: Lawrence Erlbaum, 1984).
5 M. Galton, B. Simon and P. Croll, *Inside the Primary Classroom* (London: Routledge & Kegan Paul, 1980).
6 C. Cullingford, *The Primary Teacher* (London: Cassell, 1989).
7 S.W. Percival, 'The case for a Centre for Primary Education', paper presented to the Centre for Primary Education (October 1981), p. 1.
8 Ibid.
9 S.N. Bennett, J. Andreae, P. Hegarty and B. Wade, *Open Plan Schools: Teaching, Curriculum, Design* (Slough: National Foundation for Educational Research, 1980).
10 J. Gretton, *William Tyndale: Collapse of a School or a System* (London: George Allen & Unwin, 1976).
11 Matters agreed at the final discussion of the Primary Education Study Group (what was at the time referred to as the Charlotte Mason Group), 23 April 1983.
12 Discussion of the future aims, role and organization of the Primary Education Study Group (12 November 1983).
13 C. Cullingford, *Parents, Teachers and Schools* (London: R. Royce, 1986).
14 C. Cullingford, *Parents, Education and the State* (Aldershot: Arena, 1996).
15 S.W. Percival, 'Opening Pandora's box: primary education and parents', paper presented to the Primary Education Study Group (April 1987).
16 Ibid., fn. 16.
17 From a summary of a paper on the aims of government and the role of LEAs given to the Primary Education Study Group's Manchester conference (2–3 November 1984).
18 Walter Ulrich, 'Key issues for primary education for the next five years', paper presented to the Primary Education Study Group, Ambleside (April 1983).

19 Norman Thomas, 'The trend towards close analysis', paper presented to the Primary Education Study Group, Ambleside (April 1983).

20 David Winkley and Richard Howard, 'Questions for headteachers in the 1950's', paper presented to the Primary Education Study Group, London (November 1983).

21 R.J. Alexander, 'The National Curriculum and the language of primary education', paper presented to the Primary Education Study Group, Ambleside (November 1988).

22 W. Percival, 'Opening Pandora's box', para. 6.

23 Ibid., p. 18.

24 C. Cullingford, *Parents, Education and the State* (Aldershot: Arena, 1996); M. Hughes, F. Wikeley and T. Nash, *Parents and Their Children's Schools* (Oxford: Blackwell, 1994).

25 This mythology is not confined to extreme political points of view like that of the Hillgate Group, but also taken up in anecdotal form by many politicians.

26 I. Gilmour, *Dancing with Dogma* (London: Pocket Books, 1992).

27 Department of Education and Science, *A Language for Life* (London: HMSO, 1975).

28 The ILEA survey was summarized by Norman Thomas as suggesting that there should be ten specialists in the primary school – one each for language, mathematics, science, CDT, fine arts, religious and moral education, children's literature, music, physical education, and assessment and evaluation.

29 P. Dalin, T. Ayono, A. Biazen, D. Dibara, M. Jalian, B. Matthew, M. Rojas and C. Rojac, *How Schools Improve. An International Report* (London: Cassell, 1994).

2

Early childhood education finds its voice: but is anyone listening?

Gillian Pugh

Despite the promises of the Plowden Report in 1967 and the 1972 White Paper *A Framework for Expansion*, the development of early childhood services over the last 25 years has been remarkable for its lack of vision and commitment, for the lack of cohesion in provision reflected in the continuing separation of care and education, for the gradual creeping down of the starting age of formal schooling, and for its neglect by all political parties.[1] Now that, in the final years of the century, there is a reawakening of interest in young children, we have to ask what kind of childhood we want for children in the twenty-first century, and what kind of support parents and communities are to be offered in these vital early years.

From the opening of Robert Owen's first nursery in South Lanark in 1816, and through the pioneering work of early educators such as Friedrich Froebel, Margaret McMillan, Maria Montessori and Susan Isaacs in the late nineteenth and early twentieth centuries, Britain became internationally renowned for the quality of its nursery education. And yet, as Table 2.1 shows, the development of universal nursery education has been very slow, and other services have developed to meet the needs of younger children and of their parents in balancing the demands of work and bringing up children: day nurseries, playgroups, private schools and nurseries, childminders, family centres and informal community groups. In this chapter I use the term 'early childhood education' to embrace a wide range of provision and to encompass the years from birth to age 6 as the first stage of the education system.

Despite the early pioneers, nursery education is still only available to just over a quarter of 3- and 4-year-olds, and almost all of these places are

Table 2.1 Under-fives in England: use of services, 1993

	1975	1985	1993
Places per 100 children aged 0–4			
Local authority nurseries	0.8	1.0	0.66
Private nurseries	0.8	0.8	3.42
Childminders	2.6	4.7	9.27
Places per 100 children aged 3–4			
Playgroups	23.3	33.8	30.70
Pupils as per cent of children aged 3–4			
Nursery schools and classes	10.0	22.5	26.29
Under-fives in infant classes	18.9	20.7	24.46
Independent schools	2.1	2.5	3.69

Source: Early Childhood Education Forum, *Quality in Diversity: A Framework for Early Learning for Children 0–8*, National Children's Bureau (1995), based on government statistics.

part-time – two and a half hours a day. Of 3- and 4-year-olds just under a quarter (or 85 per cent if we look just at 4-year-olds) are going early into reception classes in full-time schooling – so, in effect, the majority of children in England (and all in Northern Ireland, most in Wales, but few in Scotland) start school at 4, two years earlier than the official start of their counterparts in most other countries in the world, but actually missing out the early provision available elsewhere.

Some thirty years ago, in order to fill the gap left by an inadequate level of nursery education, the playgroup movement was set up to support parents in the provision of group activities for young children. The Preschool Learning Alliance, as the national body for playgroups has just renamed itself, now argues that playgroups should be seen not as a stopgap but as an alternative to nursery education.[2] Just under a third of this age group (the majority of them 3-year-olds) attend playgroups, where their attendance is likely to be two or three sessions a week.

But none of these alternatives provides for the needs of parents who are working or studying – now almost half of all mothers with under-fives. And so to this jigsaw of services must also be added the day nurseries run by local authorities (a dwindling service, now providing rather fewer places than in 1945, and these almost all for families experiencing difficulties); childminders caring for children in their own homes; and private nurseries, a sector which has grown dramatically in the last decade.

The discretionary nature of nursery education in Britain has thus led to a situation where there is considerable variation from one area to another, where services are provided by a range of different agencies with often very different underpinning philosophies, aims and objectives, standards and levels of staffing, and where there is a very heavy dependence on the voluntary and private sectors. This situation is in marked contrast to the position in continental Europe, where levels of public funding for pre-school services are much higher (France and Belgium have places for 95 per cent of 3- and 4-year-olds, for example, and 20 per cent of under-threes), and where public policies see the care and education of children as the responsibility of society as a whole for the citizens of tomorrow. As Moss comments: 'The United Kingdom is unique in depending so heavily on its provision for children over three in playgroups, early admission to primary school and a "shift system" for nursery education.'[3]

Blocks to progress

But why should UK policies on early childhood be so different from those of our European neighbours? This is, of course, a complex issue, but a number of different reasons can be suggested. Recent education ministers appear to have taken the view that young children are their parents' responsibility, that there is no evidence on the long-term effectiveness of early intervention, that there is uncertainty as to what is required, and that in any case we cannot afford it.[4] Politicians of all parties have been reluc-tant to encourage the state to intervene in family life, preferring to wait until a crisis has been reached before providing support. And the long shadow of the writings of John Bowlby on bonding, attachment and separ-ation have had a tenacious hold on the psyche of a country where many still interpret his work as supporting the view that mothers should be at home looking after their children.[5] This is evident, for example in the Plowden Report, which argued: 'Some mothers who are not obliged to work may work full time, regardless of their children's welfare. It is no business of the educational service to encourage these mothers to do so.'[6]

Perhaps another reason for the neglect is that the care and education of young children, and the balancing of responsibilities for work and home, are still predominantly seen as women's issues. At both national and local level, few politicians have taken this seriously. Early childhood educators seldom reach positions from which they are able to influence decisions about meeting the needs of young children – whether as primary head teachers, senior advisers and inspectors, chief education officers, senior Civil Servants or members of Parliament. The rare exceptions prove the rule – for example, significant developments in New Zealand followed the publication of an early years policy document[7] written by the chief adviser to the education minister (who was also prime minister), an early years specialist who is now director of the New Zealand Council for Educational Research.

The very early starting age for school has also militated against the establishment of a coherent and integrated nursery curriculum. Most countries in Europe start school at 6 or 7, and have a three-year kinder-garten or nursery stage from 3 to 6. If children of 4 in Britain are already in classes where teachers are teaching to the National Curriculum, it becomes increasingly difficult to look at the specific requirements of an early years curriculum which is planned with the learning needs of young children in mind.

But perhaps the greatest barrier to developing early education has been the lack of clarity over what is needed and why, reinforced by the division of responsibility for service provision between different government departments. The diversity of services noted above has led to different ser-vices being used by different families for different purposes: social ser-vices day nurseries for children 'in need'; private nurseries and childminders for working parents; nursery education and playgroups for children whose parents can use part-time places. So what are we calling for and why?

- Are we arguing for a better start for children as they enter formal school-ing?[8]
- Or for day care to enable parents to work?[9]
- Are we calling for stimulation and challenge at a time when a child's brain is developing so swiftly?[10]
- Are we driven by the arguments for equal opportunities for women?[11]
- Are we supporting employers' realization that it is more costly to recruit new staff than to provide child care for their existing staff?[12]
- Are we arguing for the need to reduce the benefits bill and enable single parents to find work?[13]
- Are we seeking to intervene to prevent or alleviate developmental delay and handicapping conditions?[14]
- Or are we trying to provide a safety net and parent education for vulner-able families, in order to prevent later juvenile delinquency?[15]
- Should we press for well-trained teachers or argue that parents are their children's first educators and that playgroups are the answer,[16] or that anyone can teach young children (as in government's 'Mums army' pro-posals that younger children could be taught by teacher assistants)?

With such a range of arguments – all of them put forward with great con-viction over the last ten years – it is no wonder that it has been possible to ignore the voices who argue for the effectiveness of early childhood edu-cation altogether.

The climate changes

Before discussing the view that the state cannot afford early childhood education, that anyone can teach young children, and that politicians do not know what is required, it is necessary to look for any evidence of the effectiveness of early education.

A series of influential reports over the last few years have built up a coherent case for the importance of investment in early childhood education for educational, social and economic reasons, thus drawing together many of these sometimes divergent arguments. The first of these was a report in 1989 from the House of Commons Education Select Committee, which argued for an increase in nursery education and for an end to the practice of early school entry for children of 4, emphasizing the value of nursery education here and now rather than just as a preparation for school:

> The case for education for under fives should not be put in terms of the longer term benefits alone. While it is clearly important that children have these [academic and social] skills to enter school and that the foundation is firm and sound for future schooling, preschool education is important and is a valid stage in itself. It is not merely a preparation for something else, but caters for the children's needs at the time and may be justified in those terms.[17]

The government's response to this report was to set up another committee, to look not at expansion but at the quality of the educational experiences of children aged 3 and 4. In its report, *Starting with Quality*, this committee, chaired by Angela Rumbold, argued that where children learn, how they learn and how they feel when they are learning are as important as what they learn.[18] Unlike more recent documents (for example, the School Curriculum and Assessment Authority (SCAA) consultation paper on activities and outcomes for 4-year-olds),[19] the report based its recommendations on an understanding of how young children learn (with a particularly strong emphasis on playing and talking) and of the critical role of well-trained adults in taking that learning forward:

> Early years educators play a critical role in young children's learning. It is within their power to encourage feelings of fun and discovering in learning on the one hand, or of dull drudgery on the other. Attitudes and behaviour patterns established during the first years of life are central to future educational and social development. Particular attention has thus to be given in these early years to the process by which a child acquires the disposition to learn and necessary competencies for learning.[20]

The report argued that there should be comparable quality in all settings in which young children find themselves and placed a heavy emphasis on the skills, knowledge and attitudes required by teachers and other early childhood educators. The term 'educator' was deliberately chosen, for 'education for the under fives can happen in a wide variety of settings and can be supplied by a wide range of people. Some will be professional teachers; many will not.'[21]

The Rumbold Report was greeted by official silence, but was received with much enthusiasm by those working in the field. Countless working parties within local authorities have used the report as the starting point for developing their own curriculum guidelines, and the thinking has also fed into the national Quality in Diversity project which is outlined below.[22]

The issues of levels of provision and of the need for a national strategy were taken up by the Equal Opportunities Commission, which called for the creation of a national day-care development agency under the aegis of the Department of Education and Science;[23] and by the Association of Metropolitan Authorities, which argued for an integration of all early childhood services.[24] The National Children's Bureau used its own outline of what a national policy should comprise[25] to commission an economist to estimate what a comprehensive system of day care and early education would cost and how it could be funded.[26] More recently, the National Commission on Education placed the expansion of nursery education as its highest priority in its reflections on the future of education and training in the UK;[27] and the Royal Society of Arts (RSA) described the situation in the UK as a 'national disgrace' and argued for the raising of the school starting age to 6, with part-time nursery education for all children aged 3 to 5.[28]

All of these reports show a growing awareness of practice elsewhere in Europe. The data showing the UK languishing towards the bottom of tables comparing public investment in early childhood services across the European Union,[29] together with a greater cross-fertilization of research and practice between Britain and her European neighbours, have also served to strengthen the arguments for a higher level of investment in this phase of education.

The effectiveness of early learning

Both the National Commission and the RSA drew on papers prepared by Sylva and colleagues,[30] which reviewed the research on the impact of early learning on children's later development. Sylva quotes American and British research to argue that early learning experiences have immediate, measurable gains on the cognitive and social development of pre-school children, and that there is a strong case for investment in high-quality learning on economic as well as social grounds. The most widely quoted study (and perhaps the one that finally persuaded the UK government to increase its investment in early education) is the longitudinal High Scope research which showed that by the time the pre-schoolers reached the age of 27, for every $1000 invested, some $7000 had been or would be returned to society, through reductions in juvenile delinquency, remedial education, income support and reduced joblessness.[31] There have been no comparable research studies in the UK either in terms of rigour or of length. However, studies of performance on Standard Assessment Tasks and teacher assessments of children aged 7 showed that those who had had nursery education performed significantly better in maths and English than those with no nursery experience.[32]

But an equally important, though less well-understood, message from this research is that only high-quality pre-school education leads to lasting gains, which it does

> through encouraging high aspirations, motivation to learn and feelings of task efficacy, especially for children from disadvantaged backgrounds. It is suggested that preschool education is effective because it shapes the cognitions that children construct for explaining success and failure in school. Early learning can foster the belief in children that attainment is not innate but is, instead, achieved in part by effort.[33]

While the cumulative impact of these reports appears to have made some impact on the policies of the three main political parties, the debate has still largely been about nursery education for children of 3 and 4. The National Commission and RSA reports make passing reference to the care and education of children under 3, and the care of 3- and 4-year-olds, before and after the school day, but saw this as beyond their brief. This raises two issues. First, for many parents and children, a session of two and a half hours is simply not enough, and indeed many children – often those whose families who are most disadvantaged – are prevented from attending nursery classes because the hours do not suit their parents. Second, this narrow emphasis (made even narrower by the debate on vouchers for 4-year-olds) ignores the growing body of evidence of the vital importance of the first three years of a child's life. New research on brain formation and development, and on the impact of social and environmental factors on changes in brain structure and functioning, reaffirms the importance of an enriched early environment.[34] This is not to say that institutional responses are always the most appropriate, but rather to point to the limitations of an early childhood education strategy that is only concerned with 4- and sometimes 3-year-olds and does not include consideration of the role of parents as their children's first educators, and of the relationships between parents and early childhood educators.

We can afford it

The evidence summarized by Sylva makes the educational, social and financial case for investment. In a reworking of her original costings to take account of legislative and demographic changes, Holtermann argues that we can also afford to make the investment.[35] She estimates that the combined package of free nursery education for 3- and 4-year-olds, together with subsidized day care which parents would pay for according to their means, would amount to additional public spending of £2.7 billion. However, the savings from women coming off benefits, and the income tax and national insurance contributions of additional women in employment, would amount to more than enough to cover all additional expenditure. As Moss argues, the issue is not one of funding, but of priorities and lack of political will:

> Ministers have offered an unconvincing and inadequate defence of the status quo, by setting a high value on diversity (at the expense of quality, effectiveness and choice), by expressing doubt about the value of preschool education (in the face of evidence of research and the experience of other countries), and by trusting in the private sector (without ensuring both that those most in need – and most likely to benefit – will thereby be provided for) and that the provision will be of statutory quality.[36]

Clearly, universal early childhood education could be afforded, but it would mean either an increased education budget overall (as the National Commission recommended) or a shift within the education budget from higher education to the early years (as the RSA report argued for).

What is early childhood education, and how should it be provided?

But what of the uncertainty as to what is required or as to whether trained teachers are really needed to provide it? What progress has been made on these issues?

Although the views below are my own, I have been much influenced by my involvement over the last three years as chair of the Early Childhood Education Forum, a consortium of the 40 major national organizations concerned with the care and education of young children. Member organizations represent statutory provision in education and social services, the voluntary and private sectors, services for children with special educational needs, parents, governors, advisers, inspectors and local authorities. Set up during the passage through Parliament of what was to become the 1993 Education Act, the Forum's overriding concern has been to bring these very disparate groups together to speak with one voice on behalf of young children. While each organization obviously wishes to emphasize a particular aspect of early years work, the Forum's overall aims have been to achieve together what none has succeeded in achieving alone: greater public awareness of the needs of young children; a more appropriate share of resources for early years services; common standards across all services; and appropriate training for all early childhood educators. The Forum's underpinning principles are as follows:

- that young children are important in their own right, and as a resource for the future;
- that young children are valued and their full development is possible only if they live in an environment which reflects and respects their individual identity, culture and heritage;
- that parents are primarily responsible for nurturing and supporting the development of their children and that this important role should be more highly valued by society;
- that central and local government have a duty, working in partnership with parents, to ensure that services and support are available for families: services that encourage children's cognitive, social, emotional and physical development; and meet parents need for support for themselves and day care for their children.[37]

With regard to children's learning, the member organizations of the Forum believe that:

- education begins at birth;
- care and education are inseparable – quality care is educational, and quality education is caring;
- every child develops at her own pace, but that adults can stimulate and encourage learning;
- all children benefit from developmentally appropriate care and education;
- skilled and careful observation is the key to helping children to learn;
- cultural and physical diversity should be respected and valued: a proactive anti-bias approach should be adopted and stereotypes challenged;
- learning is holistic and cannot be compartmentalized: trust, motivation, interest, enjoyment and social skills are as important as purely cognitive gains;
- young children learn best through first-hand experience, through play and through talk;
- carers and educators should work in partnership with parents, who are their children's first educators;
- quality care and education require well-trained educators/carers and ongoing training and support.

These principles are now shared by all sectors of the early childhood world and are reflected in the curriculum documents of local authorities and individual nurseries across the UK.

Having identified some of the blocks to progress on developing appropriate early childhood services in the UK, and having outlined some of the research and developments that have tried to confront these blocks, I would now like to consider the steps that I believe are necessary if we are to move forward.

A national policy framework

The starting point has to be a national policy commitment from central government, which can provide the legislative and financial support to ensure that all children have access to high-quality services that parents can afford. Such a policy framework can best be developed if one government department takes the lead – preferably the Department for Education and Employment if the years from birth to six are to be the first stage of the education system. It must provide medium- and long-term objectives, specific goals for levels of provision and standards to be achieved, and the resources to make them attainable. A diverse system that purports to give parents choice must be adequately funded if families on low incomes are not to be disadvantaged.

The proposals for a system of vouchers for parents of 4-year-olds are an irrelevant diversion. While the additional resources are welcome, the introduction of vouchers, largely paid for by taking money away from local authorities and recycling it to parents, in order to enable them to buy provision that is already being used free by 85 per cent of 4-year-olds, is creating an unnecessary and expensive bureaucracy, and misses an important opportunity to create a long-term policy for an integrated system of care and education. There is no evidence that a system of vouchers has worked elsewhere; the new system will make both short- and long-term planning a nightmare for local authorities and individual schools and nurseries; the highest providing authorities are likely to lose the greatest amount of provision, especially for 3-year-olds; there are serious concerns over how quality will be maintained, when the value of the voucher (£1100) is considerably less than is currently spent on a nursery education place; there is no additional money for children with special educational needs or for the training of staff; money is being taken from those who can afford least and given to those who are already paying for places; and there is utter confusion among parents – and almost everyone else – about how the system will work.

The government has made it clear that it wishes expansion to be through the private and voluntary sectors. The Early Childhood Education Forum has consistently argued that if this is to be the case, a more equitable way of ensuring a spread of places would be to build on the Children Act requirement for a triennial review of services for children under 8 and for government to require local authorities to develop a corporate plan in association with the voluntary and private sectors.

A role for local authorities

Within this national framework there must be integrated policies and provision at local level. The proposal for a development plan noted above assumes a key role for local authorities in planning and providing education and day-care services in response to the need of local parents, and in assessing and providing for those children in need of additional support. There is also an important role in regulating and supporting voluntary sector and private providers. Studies undertaken by the National Children's Bureau of the first Children Act review[38] and of the way in which 11 local authorities organize their early childhood services[39] illustrate the potential of a more integrated approach to service planning in terms of improvements in the quality of services, better information, greater access to training and a clearer sense of purpose and direction.

Flexible, high-quality services

But what kind of early education services do parents want and children need if, as I suggested earlier, part-time nursery education may not suit many parents, and early entry into school may not be appropriate for many children? Surveys of parents' views over many years show a continuing preference for nursery education over playgroups, and for more day-care and after-school and holiday provision.[40] They ask for reliable standards, for facilities located near where they live or work and flexible enough to meet changing needs, and for better information about what services are available.[41] However, there is likely to be considerable variation from one area to another. A wrap-around project in four schools in Birmingham, for example, discovered that many parents wanted somewhere to meet and access to training, rather than extra day care.[42] Most studies, however, point to the importance of flexibility, and often the need for more than two and a half hours a day.

It is this parental demand for more hours, together with concern about summer-born children falling behind their peers, and schools wanting to fill empty places, that has led a growing number of local authorities to take children into reception classes of primary schools at the beginning (rather than the end) of the year in which they become 5. While some authorities have invested a considerable amount in additional training and staffing, there is now very clear evidence that there are no educational or behavioural advantages in entering school early, and a growing body of research which shows the adverse effects of introducing children too early to an inappropriately formal curriculum.[42] Studies have found that less than a quarter of teachers in reception classes are trained to work with children of this age,[43] and the curriculum and teacher–pupil ratio are often far from appropriate. These extracts from a report of provision for 4-year-olds in Sheffield are typical of many such reports:

> There is often a stark contrast for four year olds between their experiences in the nursery class and those in the first reception setting, even in the same school. Curriculum continuity and progression in this respect is frequently poor . . .
>
> In many rising fives and reception classes the perceived demands of the National Curriculum dominate planning and lead to an inappropriate curriculum . . .
>
> In most rising five and reception classes there is an over-emphasis on the acquisition of formal skills and recording on paper at the expense of first hand experiences and exploratory activities. The status of many informal and practical activities is low and these activities are often relegated to time left over from formal tasks and frequently lack teacher intervention . . . Many children waste time on low level tasks and are insufficiently challenged . . .
>
> There is helpful stability [of staff] in nursery settings but in rising five and reception classes there are significant concerns as budgetary constraints make temporary appointments an imperative for schools.[45]

Current funding arrangements and the lack of day-care provision are conspiring to encourage many schools to make inappropriate provision for their youngest children. Surely the best way forward for children and their families would be to raise the starting age for formal schooling to 6, and for every school to provide an early childhood unit, either on its own premises or by linking with local playgroups, childminders, private nurseries and out-of-school schemes. Such a unit would provide nursery education for children from 3 to 6, and day care for younger children, before- and after-school and holiday activities for all primary children, drop-in facilities for parents and childminders, a child health clinic, support for parents and a community focus that is badly needed in many communities. Many school buildings are open for only a relatively small proportion of the year, and hold tremendous potential as the focus for an integrated early childhood service.[46]

A key factor in high-quality early childhood education is an appropriate curriculum, and the earlier quotations from the Rumbold Report and

Sylva's summary of research point to key factors in such a curriculum. The Rumbold Report argued that 'educators should guard against pressures which might lead them to over-concentration on formal teaching and upon the attainment of a specific set of targets'.[48] An analysis of the curriculum frameworks developed by a considerable number of local authorities points to the importance of a broad developmental curriculum which responds to children's interests and concerns as expressed in their persistent activities seeing play as the means by which children understand and gain control over their environment, their feelings and experiences, and their learning.

The Early Childhood Education Forum's *Quality in Diversity* project[49] is creating a framework for children's learning from birth to 8. It has been developed by all 40 member organizations and is based on five foundations:

- Being and becoming: effective learning begins with self-respect, feelings of personal worth and identity; it includes care of self, and the health and safety of the individual.
- Belonging and connecting: effective learning involves developing good relationships with other children and with adults, in families, communities and group settings; it involves learning to be a member of a child's own linguistic and cultural community group.
- Being active and expressive: effective learning involves young children in being both physically and mentally active. They are stimulated to express their own ideas by the many encounters and experiences that engage their interest.
- Contributing and participating: effective learning includes contributing to others in various ways, learning when to lead and when to support leaders, learning to be responsible for self and others and to make appropriate choices in a group. Contributing and participating are motivated by a sense of belonging.
- Thinking, imagining and reflecting: in order to learn effectively children build up their own understanding through the active processes of thinking, imagining and reflecting on everything they experience. These processes are crucial to real understanding and to positive attitudes to learning.

This approach, which includes clear links into National Curriculum subjects, areas of experience as outlined by Her Majesty's Inspectorate[50] and the High/Scope and Montessori curricula, seems far more appropriate to young children's learning than the proposals published by SCAA[51] which reduce development to a low level and narrow band of outcomes and seriously underestimate young children's power and capacity to think. As the quotation from the Rumbold Report above makes clear, young children's learning is not just about skills and knowledge, but is integral to their social and emotional development and to their developing the disposition to learn.

Parents as educators

Children are learning from the moment they are born – or even before – and their parents and wider family provide both the context in which this learning takes place and the continuity between home, pre-school and school. As children move into early education or day-care settings their learning will continue to be strongly influenced by the home environment, and the closer the links between parents and nursery, playgroup or child-minder, the more effective that learning will be.

Lip-service has been paid to the key role that parents play in their children's education ever since Bronfenbrenner's overview of US Headstart programmes in 1974 concluded that 'strategies which included parents in early childhood education seemed to be more effective in terms of long term gains that those which did not', and the National Children's Bureau's National Child Development Study's report for the Plowden Committee argued that 'the variation in parental attitudes can account for more of the variations in children's school achievement that either the variation in home circumstances or in schools'.[52] As Woodhead points out in his analysis of the implications of the High Scope research for Britain, improved early performance, higher teacher expectations, increased pupil motivation and increased parental aspirations become mutually reinforcing.[53] Pre-school programmes, he argues, are 'powerful in engineering, reinforcing and sustaining parental aspirations and interest in their children's education'.

However, if we consider the new evidence cited above about the importance of the first three years, taken together with studies which show the enormous potential of the home as a learning environment,[54] then the links between parents, schools and other community workers such as health visitors become increasingly important. Studies of parental involvement in early education[55] illustrate both the extent of the barriers that schools can erect, albeit unwittingly, between themselves and parents, but also the potential of those approaches that enable, facilitate and empower parents to participate in their children's education. Initiatives such as the Home Early Learning Project (HELP) in Leeds,[56] the East Moulsecoomb Preschool project,[57] Athey's study of involving parents in observing their children's development alongside their teachers,[58] the Sheffield REAL (Raising Early Achievement in Literacy (REAL) project[59]) and the Peers Early Education Project in Oxford[60] all illustrate what can be achieved by working alongside parents and involving them in their children's learning.

How should early childhood educators be trained?

It is sometimes asserted that 'anyone can teach young children', and yet anyone who has spent a day with a group of lively, curious 3- or 4-year-olds will know what a skilled and demanding job it is. The RSA report argues that early years teachers require a breadth of knowledge, understanding and experience which is not needed by those training to teach older children:

> They must have mastery of the curriculum content as well as having a sound knowledge of child development, including language acquisition, cognitive, social, emotional and physical development. They are required to lead and plan for a team of other professionals including parents, nursery nurses, students, and others including speech therapists, language support teachers, psychologists and social workers. They are responsible for the assessment of children and for monitoring progress and ensuring continuity and progression between stages and establishments.[61]

The quality of children's education depends to a large extent on the quality of the teachers and other adults working with them, and yet the majority of those working with children under 5 in the private and voluntary sectors are not formally qualified – although they may be very experienced – and their pay and status are very low. As noted above, of those who are trained as teachers many working in reception classes are not trained to work with children of this age, and there is growing concern about the appropriateness of primary teacher training, with its continuing emphasis on subject specialism and its neglect of child development.

Opportunities for further training are often limited. The system of National Vocational Qualifications in child care and education offered the promise of accreditation to many, but work at level 3 is still incomplete, while work on level 4 has not even started. Becoming accredited is also a costly business, beyond the means of many on very low wages.

It seems curious that in the current debate about expanding education for 4-year-olds there has been much discussion about a 'light touch' inspection service, but absolutely no mention of training. There are to be no qualification requirements within the institutions that may redeem vouchers – despite the emphasis on this being an education initiative – and no additional funding for continuing in-service training. The Early Childhood Education Forum has argued that all managers of centres, nurseries or playgroups should be graduates or hold NVQ level 4 or equivalent, and all who work in centres or as childminders should be at level 3. But with no national programme of early years training and cutbacks in the number of early years teacher training places, we will be well into the twenty-first century before this is achieved.

Initial training is important, but so too is a culture of continuous training, reflection and staff development. The balance between inspection on the one hand and staff development and training on the other would seem to have swung rather too strongly away from training and support, and if quality is to be developed and maintained, this balance will need to be redressed. Initiatives such as the Principles into Practice project at Goldsmiths College[62] and the Effective Early Learning Project at Worcester College of Higher Education should be part of mainstream funding rather than dependent on charitable trusts and enthusiastic individuals.[63]

In conclusion

After years of official neglect, there now appears to be growing acceptance of research that shows that it is during the first five years that the foundations for all later learning are laid, and a greater willingness to accept that investment at this stage can be justified. The official spotlight has fallen on children of 4, and there has been a more vocal public debate about how young children learn, about what is an appropriate curriculum, about how early years educators should be trained, and about the role that parents play in their children's learning.

This debate is to be welcomed but, as I have argued in this chapter, it is still limited in scope and often misguided in focus. 'Pre-school' education is not only about preparation for school, but also about meeting the needs of young children here and now, about responding to their innate curiosity and enthusiasm, about helping them to develop motivation, persistence, concentration and the disposition to learn. It is not only about 4-year-olds or appropriate outcomes; but also about the care and education of all children in the first five years of their lives, and about the partnerships that need to be forged between early childhood educators and parents if children's learning is to be supported. And it is about training a professional workforce, recognizing the breadth of skills, knowledge and understanding required to work effectively with young children.

The attempts by national early childhood organizations to speak with one voice on these issues have been put under severe strain by the current stress on a market-place economy, where diverse providers in the private and voluntary sectors are being encouraged to compete with local authorities in providing nursery education. While services still fall so far short of what is required, this seems an unhelpful and short-sighted approach. At a local level, partnerships between providers will be required if the needs of children and parents are to be met, and the critical role of nursery teachers and advisers will need to be acknowledged and supported. Education does not only happen in nursery classes, but trained nursery teachers have an important part to play, both in sharing their expertise with other early childhood educators in schools, playgroups and private nurseries, and in providing the firm foundations within the school upon which the rest of children's education is built.

The last few years have seen a much greater consensus among those who work with young children and those who manage and plan for their services as to what is needed and how it should be achieved, but there is little evidence that the government is listening. If there is genuine commitment to increasing educational opportunities for young children, then there has to be a recognition that this requires the necessary legislative and financial infrastructure to support and develop quality services, and a culture in which children are respected and their rights acknowledged and respected.

Notes

1 Central Advisory Council for Education (CACE), *Children and Their Primary Schools* (London: HMSO, 1967); Department of Education and Science (DES), *Teacher Education: A Framework for Expansion* (London: HMSO, 1972).
2 Preschool Playgroups Association, *Playgroups: The Way Forward* (London: PPA, 1994).
3 P. Moss, 'Statistics in Early Childhood Services: Placing Britain in an International Context' in C. Ball (ed.), *Start Right: The Importance of Early Learning* (London: Royal Society of Arts, 1994), p. 113.
4 House of Commons Education, Science and Arts Committee, *Educational Provision for the Under Fives: First Report*, session 1988–89 (London: HMSO, 1989).
5 J. Bowlby, *Attachment* (London: Hogarth Press, 1982).
6 CACE, *Children and Their Primary Schools*.
7 New Zealand Department of Education, *Education To Be More*, Report of the Early Childhood Care and Education Working Group (Wellington: Department of Education, 1988).
8 House of Commons Education, Science and Arts Committee, *Educational Provision for the Under Fives: First Report*; Department of Education and Science (DES), *Starting with Quality*, Report of the (Rumbold) Committee of Enquiry into the Educational Experiences Offered to Three and Four Years Olds (London: HMSO, 1990).
9 S. Holtermann and K. Clarke, *Parents, Employment Rights and Childcare* (London: Equal Opportunities Commission, 1992).
10 Carnegie Corporation, *Starting Points: Meeting the Needs of Our Youngest Children* (New York: Carnegie Corporation, 1994).
11 Equal Opportunities Commission, *The Key to Real Choice* (London: EOC, 1990).
12 Business in the Community, *Corporate Culture and Caring: The Business Case for Fairly Friendly Provision* (London: Institute of Personnel Management, 1993).
13 S. Holtermann, *Investing in Young Children: Costing an Education and Day Care Service* (London: National Children's Bureau, 1992); S. Holtermann, *Investing in Young Children: A Reassessment of the Cost of an Education and Day Care Service* (London: National Children's Bureau, 1995).
14 B. Carpenter (ed.), *Early Intervention: Where Are We Now?* (Oxford: Westminster College, 1994).

15 D. Utting, J. Bright and C. Henricson, *Crime and the Family: Improving Child Rearing and Preventing Delinquency* (London: Family Policy Studies Centre, 1993).
16 Preschool Playgroups Association, *Playgroups*.
17 House of Commons Education, Science and Arts Committee, *Educational Provision for the Under Fives: First Report*.
18 DES, *Starting with Quality*.
19 School Curriculum and Assessment Authority, *Preschool Education Consultation. Desirable Outcomes for Children's Learning and Guidance for Providers* (London: SCAA, 1995).
20 DES, *Starting with Quality*, p. 36.
21 DES, *Starting with Quality*, p. 39.
22 Early Childhood Education Forum, *Quality in Diversity: A Framework for Early Learning for Children 0–8* (London: National Children's Bureau, 1995).
23 EOC, *The Key to Real Choice*.
24 Association of Metropolitan Authorities, *Children First* (London: AMA, 1991).
25 Under Fives Unit, *A Policy for Under Fives: A Framework for Action* (London: National Children's Bureau, 1990).
26 Holtermann, *Investing in Young Children* (1992).
27 National Commission on Education, *Learning to Succeed* (London: Heinemann, 1993).
28 P. Moss, 'Statistics on Early Childhood Services: Placing Britain in an International Context', in Ball, *Start Right*.
29 Ibid.; G. Pugh (ed.), *Contemporary Issues in the Early Years*, 2nd edn (London: Paul Chapman, 1996).
30 See, for example, K. Sylva, 'The Impact of Early Learning on Children's Later Development', in Ball, *Start Right*.
31 L. Schweinhart and D. Weikart, *A Summary of Significant Benefits: the High/Scope Perry Preschool Study through Age 27* (Washington, DC: High/Scope, 1993).
32 I. Schagen, 'Multilevel analysis of the Key Stage 1 National Curriculum assessment data in 1991 and 1992', *Oxford Review of Education*, 21(2), 163–78 (1995); S. Daniels, 'Can pre-school education affect children's achievement in primary school?', *Oxford Review of Education*, 21(2), 163–78 (1995).
33 Sylva, 'The Impact of Early Learning'.
34 Carnegie, *Starting Points*; H. Gardner, *The Unschooled Mind* (New York: Basic Books, 1991).
35 Holtermann, *Investing in Young Children* (1995).
36 P. Moss 'Statistics in Early Childhood Services: Placing Britain in an International Context', in Ball, *Start Right*.
37 Under Fives Unit, *A Policy for Under Fives*.
38 P. Elfer and S. McQuail, *Local Wishes and Expectations* (London: National Children's Bureau, 1995).
39 S. McQuail and G. Pugh, *Effective Organisation of Early Childhood Services* (London: National Children's Bureau, 1995).
40 H. Meltzer, *Day Care Services for Children: A Survey Carried out on Behalf of the Department of Health in 1990* (London: HMSO, 1994).
41 Holtermann, *Investing in Young Children* (1995); Elfer and McQuail, *Local Wishes and Expectations*.
42 Birmingham City Council, *The Wrap-around Project Final Report* (Birmingham: Birmingham City Council, 1996).

43 M.M. Clark, *Children under Five: Educational Research and Evidence* (London: Gordon and Breach, 1988); S. Cleave and S. Brown, *Four Year Olds in School: Meeting Their Needs* (Slough: National Foundation for Educational Research, 1989); Department of Education and Science, *A Survey of the Quality of Education of Four Year Olds in Primary Classes*, Report by HMI (London: HMSO, 1989); Ofsted, *First Class: The Standards and Quality of Education in Reception Classes* (London: HMSO, 1993); Early Years Curriculum Group, *Four Year Olds in School: Myths and Realities*, Action Paper 2 (London: Early Years Curriculum Group, 1995).

44 G. Blenkin and N. Yue, 'Profiling early years practitioners: some first impressions from a national survey', *Early Years*, 15(1), 13–22 (1994).

45 Sheffield City Council, *1994/95 Review of Education Provision for Four Year Olds in Sheffield* (Sheffield: Quality Assurance Services, 1995).

46 For further exploration of this concept, see McQuail and Pugh, *Effective Organisation of Early Childhood Services*; J. Rea Price and G. Pugh, *Championing Children. A Report for Manchester City Council* (Manchester: Manchester City Council, 1995); P. Moss and A. Pence (eds), *Valuing Quality in Early Childhood Services* (London: Paul Chapman, 1994); P. Moss and H. Penn, *Transforming Nursery Education* (London: Paul Chapman, 1996).

47 DES, *Starting with Quality*; Sylva, 'The Impact of Early Learning'.

48 DES, *Starting with Quality*, p. 23.

49 Early Childhood Education Forum, *Quality in Diversity: A Framework for Early Learning for Children 0–8* (London: National Children's Bureau, 1996).

50 DES, *Starting with Quality*.

51 SCAA, *Preschool Education Consultation*.

52 See U. Bronfenbrenner, 'The experimental ecology of education', *Teachers College Record*, 78(2), 157–204 (1974); National Children's Bureau, *National Child Development Study* (London: HMSO, 1964).

53 M. Woodhead, 'Preschool education has long-term effects: but can they be generalised?', *Oxford Review of Education*, 11(2), 133–5 (1985).

54 See, for example, B. Tizard and M. Hughes, *Young Children Learning* (London: Fontana, 1994).

55 See G. Pugh and E. De'Ath, *Working towards Partnership in the Early Years* (London: National Children's Bureau, 1989); G. Pugh, E. De'Ath and C. Smith, *Confident Parents, Confident Children: Policy and Practice in Parent Education and Support* (London: National Children's Bureau, 1994).

56 Home Early Learning Project, *Final Evaluation Report June 1995* (Leeds: Education 2000, 1995).

57 B. Daines and G. Gill, *Playlink Schemes – an Evaluation* (Lewes: East Sussex County Council, 1993).

58 C. Athey, *Extending Thought in Young Children* (London: Paul Chapman, 1990).

59 P. Hannon, 'The Sheffield REAL project', *Literacy Today*, 3, 10–11 (1995).

60 R. Roberts and W. Laar, *Peers Early Education Project Development Plan* (Oxford: Oxford County Council, 1995).

61 Ball, *Start Right*, p. 59.

62 Blenkin and Yue, 'Profiling early years practitioners'.

63 C. Pascal, T. Bertram and F. Ramsden, *Effective Early Learning: The Quality Evaluation and Development Process* (London: Amber Publishing, 1994).

3

The market experiment

Philip Hunter

A great experiment started in the 1980s. For a decade the education service in England and Wales has been put through a series of changes which were, in the eyes of the government, to transform a sloppy and complacent profession into a sharp and effective force for a better future. For too long, the Education Service had been left to the professionals, steeped in a culture of 1960s public service. It was time to sweep that away. It was time to strip the education establishment of the power it had exercised for so long and to give that power to the parents for whom the service was supposed to be provided.

The vehicle for this change was to be the market. The system was to be businesslike and mechanistic. There were four pillars on which the market system was to be built. First, the government was to draw up a contract. This was to be the National Curriculum, setting out in detail what was to be taught and how much should be learned at each stage of education. Like all contracts, it was to be in a form that left little room for doubt as to what was to be expected and allowed the work to be checked to see if it had been carried out according to specification.

Second, the contract was to be published and tenders were to be invited from independent schools. In order to drive down costs and to raise standards, it was essential to see that bids were submitted by truly independent businesses. There was to be no collusion, no cartel of suppliers who came together (or were joined together by an overarching authority) to fix prices or exercise undue influence over the way in which contracts were carried out.

Third, these efficient businesses were to reap the rewards of all successful ventures. They would expand, attracting more and more customers and hence be able to employ more staff. Their income would justify higher pay for those who worked in them, particularly for the senior managers who provided the leadership and enterprise. There would be more comfortable conditions, with carpets, curtains and bright decorations. There would be room to invest in equipment which could be more attractive to future customers and more likely to allow present customers to succeed. Conversely, bad schools would not attract customers, would run out of money and close.

Finally, schools would be made fully accountable to their customers. Parents would be given full and accurate information so they could make informed choices. They would be told how well schools performed – particularly in externally marked examinations and tests. They would also have access to the conclusions of a rigorous inspection system to ensure that contracts had been carried out properly. The inspection system was to be truly independent, certainly not tainted by any improper relationship with the providers.

The inspection system was to start from the premise that contractors would be trying to cut corners and might deliver shoddy goods. It was to be based on the hostile assumption that business was business and that the inspectors were there to protect the clients against the possibility of receiving shoddy goods.

Shirley Williams (1976–9)

This vision of a market education system did not emerge overnight. Elements of it began to appear even before the 1979 election which brought Mrs Thatcher to power. Some of the background shifts began early in 1976 when Prime Minister James Callaghan spoke at Ruskin College of the need to open up the education system to more outside influences. The response came in three forms. The Taylor Committee was set up to inject school-based reform through the introduction of more powerful governing bodies which, it was hoped, would stand up to teachers. Shortly afterwards, Shirley Williams started to open up the 'secret garden' of the curriculum. She initiated a survey among local authorities in order to find out more about what was being taught in the nation's schools. Then, there was an attempt to remove some money from local authorities in order to set up a national scheme for in-service training of teachers. This attempt failed. The product of these developments was not to emerge until the 1980s, but the direction had been set under the Labour government.

Mark Carlisle (1979–81)

The arrival of Mark Carlisle as Secretary of State in May 1979 did not lead to a major departure from this trend. There was a gesture towards increasing competition for state schools through the establishment of an assisted places scheme which helped children from supposedly poor families to obtain places in private schools. This had little impact on the system as a whole, partly through lack of funds and partly because it had no single focus. It was presented as helping poor pupils from inner-city areas but always contained the flavour of strengthening the private sector – in particular, helping private schools in financial trouble.

The scheme satisfied none of the objectives. On a broader front, the advocates of more radical solutions were marginalized. Rhodes Boyson was put in charge of higher education, with the knowledgeable and moderate Lady Young as Minister for Schools. Stuart Sexton was brought in as an adviser to the Department but was largely ignored within it by officials and ministers. There was no general move to produce a market system. Indeed, Mark Carlisle and Janet Young had to fight very hard against bitter opposition from the Prime Minister in order to keep the work on the National Curriculum afloat. Mrs Thatcher's opposition seemed to spring from the proposition that anything Her Majesty's Inspectorate for Schools wanted was bound to be wrong. There was no concept that the National Curriculum would in the long run provide one of the pillars on which the market system would be built.

Keith Joseph (1981–6)

It was the arrival of Sir Keith Joseph as Secretary of State which first exposed the tension in the Conservative government's approach to education. Joseph had been the architect of the Thatcher market revolution – reducing the size and influence of government through deregulation and denationalization and building up the private sector so that it was the market rather than planners which determined the shape and direction of the economy. This philosophy led straight down the route of privatizing the education system and, early in the Joseph administration, the means for doing so was produced. In Ashford, Kent, an education voucher system was devised. Instead of pupils being allocated places in their local schools, each child was given a voucher with a face value equal to the cost of a place in a local school. Here was the market. The child's parents chose the school, exchanged the voucher for a school place and the school reclaimed the cost of the voucher from the local education authority (LEA). The school then used the money to run itself.

The experiment failed for three reasons. First, schools and the LEA were not ready for it. They did not know enough about how much school places cost and how to set up and run school budgets. The vouchers did not in the end have any commercial worth; they were merely pieces of paper with no more significance than an allocation letter. Second, it became clear that the system led to the same decisions about the same issues being taken by the same people. If a school was over-subscribed, it could not operate like a business and control its growth by raising prices. It had to take bureaucratic decisions on which children were admitted and which were not. Third, it became apparent that the market could not of itself raise standards. Over-subscribed schools were under no pressure to do so and schools with falling numbers of pupils did not have the means to help improve their teaching accommodation or facilities. Nothing had changed.

This led Joseph to abandon structural or financial means of raising standards and to concentrate instead on the curriculum. Hence, the Joseph administration was notable for three lasting reforms. First, Her Majesty's Inspectorate produced the 'Curriculum Matters' series of booklets which led (after a huge, lengthy and very expensive diversion in the early 1990s) to the accepted version of the National Curriculum. Second, the whole process of evaluation and testing moved on to a search, which produced some return, for criterion referencing in place of norm referencing. This was not to bear fruit for some years, but eventually led to the reform of the General Certificate of Secondary Education (GCSE) and the development of National Vocational Qualifications; these in turn led to the massive increase in tertiary and higher education. Third, he succeeded where Shirley Williams had failed in removing money from the LEAs to produce a national system for in-service training. This gave the Department direct leverage over new developments in schools. It became possible for ministers to indulge their whims in the latest fashion – from reading recovery to drugs education. These were major and substantial reforms which laid some of the ground for the market system but were not in themselves directly responsible for it.

There was a further development which was directed towards the second pillar of the market system – the liberation of schools from LEAs so they could compete freely without market regulation. This was the establishment, under the 1986 Act, of governing bodies in which the LEAs were no longer in the majority. There were to be more parents, staff and community than LEA representatives. Although there was no reference in the legislation or surrounding documents to the language of the market, choice or diversity, it was clear that the new governing bodies were to be strong enough and have the powers to act in a more vigorous and independent way than ever before.

Kenneth Baker (1986–9)

Kenneth Baker arrived in 1986 with a mission to make his name. He was given to remark after his term of office that he had achieved this by accident. When he took up his post, he was faced with a teachers' pay dispute which had rumbled on for some time. It became clear that the Treasury would not brook a settlement of this on terms acceptable to teachers without enough concessions to distinguish the settlement from demands being made by other public sector groups. It was possible to do this, and achieve an ambition which had been in the Department for years, by drawing up a teachers' contract which stipulated the annual hours for work and included five statutory days' training during which teachers were to be on duty while the children were on holiday. The training days became known as 'Baker days' and the name stuck for several years.

There was a second development. This was the proposal to establish 20 city technology colleges. These were to be new schools, built by industry with recurrent funding direct from the Department for Education. Their purpose was to stimulate LEAs to better things. They were to be flagships sailing among LEA schools, leading them to new horizons. They were to pioneer new curricular developments and demonstrate how cutting out bureaucracy would lead to better use of resources.

Meanwhile, work was going ahead to prepare the biggest Education Bill since 1944. The four pillars of the market are now becoming apparent. There was to be a statutory National Curriculum, laying down in detail what was to be taught; there were to be schools truly independent of their LEAs, stimulating more independence among LEA schools; there was to be formula funding for schools so that successful schools would receive financial rewards; and information on schools' performance was to become more readily available to parents.

Work on the National Curriculum was started almost before the ink on the Act was dry. It got off to a bad start with a consultation document prepared by officials which was written in language inaccessible to teachers. Nevertheless, its main thrusts were almost immediately embedded in legislation. There were to be National Curriculum subjects, and each was to have a set of attainment targets and programmes of study associated with it. Shortly afterwards, a group chaired by Professor Paul Black produced a paper setting out the structure for the curriculum and its assessment. The backbone of this was to be ten levels of attainment which were to become the basis for assessment. Without pausing for breath, working groups started in maths, English, science and technology to draw up the curriculum in these subjects. They were set up in sequence so there was no overall framework within which they were to fit. It was only after these groups had been wound up and others on history, geography and modern languages were started that it became apparent that the working groups were not sticking to the piece of canvas on which they had been asked to paint.

The second pillar was the establishment of independent, free-standing schools competing for custom. The city technology notion had clearly failed. Industry was simply not interested nor prepared to pay. A few were started with contributions from sympathetic entrepreneurs but even these had to receive large subsidies from central government. Some of them were started in locations where there was already a local surplus of school places. The whole process was struggling. The answer to this was to be grant-maintained schools. These were schools which already existed under LEA control but were to be allowed to 'opt out', becoming independent corporate bodies receiving funding direct from central government. They would be rather like the direct-grant grammar schools which were abandoned by the Labour government in the early 1970s. Again the emphasis was on large schools with more than 300 pupils which would become flagships. The Department was keen to emphasize to ministers that they should pick winners and not get themselves landed with schools needing attention. They were still heavily reliant on the catalytic effect that the few schools would have on the mass. LEAs would be likely to remove the shackles from their own schools in order to reduce the likelihood that those schools would choose to opt out completely.

The third pillar was the overt relationship between pupil numbers and school finance. Most schools were already funded on the basis of a set of formulae. Usually there was a separate formula for staffing, capitation and buildings maintenance. Some authorities – principally ILEA and Cambridgeshire – had experimented with extending this to allow funds dedicated for one purpose to be reallocated to another. The legislation required LEAs to go further. Schools were to be given a budget covering 80 per cent of their costs and asked to take complete responsibility for the way this money was to be spent. Crucially, budgets were to be calculated using a formula which was applied equally to all schools. Thus the link between funding and pupil numbers was direct; the language of 'units of resource' and 'age-weighted pupil units' emerged, leading to some direct comparisons between this scheme and the voucher scheme which had been tried in the early 1980s.

The fourth pillar was information for parents to allow them to play the market. School performance had long been seen by Conservative ministers as capable of being represented in terms of results obtained in externally assessed examinations. The 1988 Act said very little about this, and it was clearly not felt then to be as prominent a part of the thinking as it later became. Nevertheless, the building blocks were being created through the assessment side of the work on the National Curriculum. This was seen as important enough to create a separate agency, the School Examination and Assessment Council (SEAC), rather than taking the ogical step of putting assessment and curricular work together. Even at this stage, therefore, there was a direct movement towards the establishment of common measures of performance and the publication of league tables showing how schools were progressing against those measures.

John MacGregor (1989–90)

The system was to experience some respite in the production of new ideas under John MacGregor, but the constant stream of development work continued. National Curriculum working groups began to produce their reports, subject by subject, with the inevitable truth gradually emerging that expecting specialist working groups to take a realistic view of the relative importance of their subject was spitting in the wind. Attempts were made by the body established to look after the new curriculum, the National Curriculum Council (NCC), to contain this, with very little success. Thicker and thicker documents started landing on teachers' desks, setting out in great detail what they were to teach. Unfortunately, many of these had to be withdrawn and reissued as the thinking progressed.

Meanwhile, SEAC too was beginning to face an old conundrum: some of what is learned in schools is simple and cheap to test, while some is complex and expensive; yet the difficult and expensive is as important as the cheap and simple. Moreover, results of cheap and simple tests are easy to present in an accessible form to parents. How much of the limited resources available for teaching is it worth taking out to provide a reasonable assessment system?

While these debates were progressing there was a small but significant change in the legislation on opting out. MacGregor came under pressure to extend the opportunity to opt out to small schools, and he announced his intention to do so at the Conservative Party conference in 1990. Grant-maintained schools were no longer to be large secondary flagships. They were to include small primary schools. The assumption was no longer to be that only schools which were unlikely to get into trouble would choose to opt out. The Department was beginning to accept that it would be landed with a major administrative task.

Kenneth Clarke (1990–2)

Kenneth Clarke came from the Department of Health with a ready-made philosophy of the internal market. He had set up hospital trusts and given general practitioners budgets with which they were able to purchase services. The parallels with education were clear.

By the time Clarke was appointed, one of the market system pillars, the curriculum, was reasonably well bedded in. His attack was on the other three – the establishment of independent units, rewarding successful schools and individuals in them, and the production of information for parents. First, he speeded up the introduction of grant-maintained schools. He talked about all secondary schools opting out (and even occasionally all schools opting out). Far from taking the relaxed Mac-Gregor line of opening up choices for schools, Clarke was keen that they should all conform with his model. Before he arrived, ministers and Civil Servants were scrupulously maintaining the line that opted-out schools did not gain financially – even though there was some element of double revenue funding. Clarke openly skewed capital funding in favour of grant-maintained schools and encouraged civil servants to look for ways of favouring them in revenue too.

Second, he set about creating a direct link between the success or failure of schools and the pay of the teachers in the school. There had always been a rather tenuous relationship in that head teachers' and deputies' pay was arranged in bands according to the size of school, with larger schools attracting more responsibility allowances. This had been negotiated between LEAs and teachers' unions in an annual round of complex and often messy negotiations. A new arrangement was introduced in a new Act in 1991. A review panel, appointed by the Secretary of State, was established to recommend the rates of pay for teachers. There was direct pressure from government to make sure that there was a performance-related dimension to pay structures. The definition of 'performance' was not spelled out, but the theory at the heart of it was the following syllogism: good teachers attract pupils; more pupils brings in more money; workers in thriving schools should be rewarded; then they will be motivated to work even harder and teachers in unpopular schools will want to share their good fortune and work hard, too.

Third, he strengthened the weakest pillar of the system – information for parents. This took two forms. On the one hand, he started pushing hard to publish league tables of examination results. This did not need legislation. Schools were already required to publish their results in a standard form, although it was difficult for parents to make direct comparisons without some research and inconvenience. Clarke wanted to make comparisons much easier. He could have done this by requiring the LEAs, most of which collected the results already and spent a great deal of effort analysing and discussing them with their schools, to publish the results on his behalf. However, he decided to go direct to the examination boards and gather the results centrally rather than risk confrontation with the LEAs.

The other means of informing parents led to one of the most significant and expensive reforms in the series. LEAs had traditionally shared the task of inspecting schools with Her Majesty's Inspectorate (HMI). Most of them employed a mixture of techniques, from visits to full inspections, which they regarded as satisfying their duty under Section 8 of the 1944 Education Act to ensure there were sufficient places (of acceptable quality) for the children who lived in their area. HMI conducted full inspections, the results of which were published.

Clarke produced a new Act to change all of this – the 1992 Education Act. In the event, the primary legislation did not make much difference. He started by trying to transfer the responsibility for ensuring an adequate inspection programme from the Secretary of State to the schools themselves. This was defeated in the House of Lords, and the responsibility ended up with Her Majesty's Chief Inspector of Schools. The Act also set out in more detail how inspections were to be conducted, but it left a great deal to regulations and circulars. These set out the disbandment of HMI and replacement of it by a new body, the Office for Standards in Education (Ofsted), transferring resources for inspection from LEAs to Ofsted, establishing a four-year cycle of inspection and requiring inspection teams to publish their reports. In the event, most of the inspection programme was carried out by LEA inspectors under contract to Ofsted. The annual cost of the programme was £130 million. The object was to ensure that parents (the market) were supplied with a flow of professional reports on the quality of schools they could choose from.

John Patten (1992–4)

By the time John Patten became Secretary of State, the four pillars of the market were almost in place – and some of them had already started to crumble. Patten was a committed market advocate and a convinced critic of local government. He had served on Oxford City Council – a body without any education powers and very little power elsewhere – so his impression was that local authorities were a waste of time. His Minister of State, Baroness Blatch, had been chair of Cambridgeshire Education Committee but had been unseated by a *putsch* organized by the establishment Conservatives in the county. She shared Patten's sour view of LEAs.

By the time Patten got his feet under the table, the Conservatives had won their fourth election. Conservative government seemed set to last for ever and there was a spate of opting out from schools which had been hanging fire against the possibility that Labour, committed as it was to restore maintained schools to local authorities, would take power. Everything seemed set fair for a further full term of office.

Patten started vigorously. He produced a White Paper, *Choice and Diversity*, the first chapter of which he wrote himself.[1] The chapter contained an eloquent and well-argued case for the market – schools delivering the National Curriculum but able to compete with each other and reap the rewards of success. Parents would have reliable information so that they could make informed choices.

Nevertheless, the White Paper went on to create conditions which threatened one of the key elements of the market, grant-maintained schools. As the number of grant-maintained schools approached 1000, the Department had to admit that it could not handle the administration. Whatever the theories about independent schools competing in the market, a public institution running on public money would have to be administered by public servants. The schools' budgets had to be set and accounts checked. Someone had to be available to clear up the mess when one of the schools found itself in trouble. As time went on the Department was becoming sucked into this and so the White Paper, in line with the Next Steps Agency philosophy, proposed a Funding Agency for Schools to take on the task. The powers of the Funding Agency were remarkably like the powers of LEAs. In particular, it had strong planning powers, presumably so that it could interfere with the market. Patten also packed the membership of the body with supporters of the Conservative Party.

Within months of the establishment of the Funding Agency for Schools, applications for grant-maintained status dried up. Schools began to realize that they were not just 'opting out' of LEAs but were opting into the new Funding Agency. Also LEAs had begun to be better organized. They began to devolve more powers and to order their finances so that schools opting out did not gain as much financially. They also started to use capital receipts more judiciously so that the advantage for grant-maintained schools and capital building was not so marked. They began to make use of the natural inclination of head teachers and chairs of governors to share responsibility and to work together. In the face of a government which seemed more and more to be uncaring and aggressive, LEAs began to look very local, friendly and supportive.

Meanwhile, work on the curriculum was getting into difficulty too. Teachers, parents and governors were beginning to be fed up with a constant stream of advice, guidance and regulations which poured out of the NCC and SEAC. The White Paper proposed merging these two bodies into the School Curriculum and Assessment Authority. Sir Ron Dearing was appointed to chair this body with the specific brief to simplify the curriculum and to make it more manageable by schools. He did so with great skill and vigour, and the schools generally seemed pleased with the outcome. It became apparent, however, that the draft produced by this process in May 1994 looked remarkably like the 'Curriculum Matters' document which had been produced by HMI 12 years before. The language was similar, the framework was similar and, if anything, the new curriculum was less prescriptive (particularly for 14–16-year-olds) than the earlier version. Despite this there were some advances in some subjects and in primary education generally. The government felt it could live with the new version.

While these two pillars of the market were beginning to crumble, a third was standing firm. The very existence of the possibility of grant-maintained status meant that LEAs were forced into greater devolution of budgets to schools. Although the regulations about how much should be devolved did not change, many schools locally were putting pressure on their LEAs to give them the kinds of powers enjoyed by grant-maintained schools. Consequently many authorities went far beyond the needs of the regulations in what they were prepared to offer schools in their budgets. Most of them established services such as advice on the curriculum, finance and personnel as well as more direct services such as music, audio-visual aids and outdoor education as self-financing agencies which sold their services to schools. In addition, some services such as catering, grounds maintenance and cleaning became the subject of the Department of the Environment legislation which required LEAs to put these out to tender. The result was that many schools found themselves virtually as free as grant-maintained schools and could purchase services from wherever they wanted. Grant-maintained schools had had the effect they were intended to have when they were established back in the late 1980s. The existence of a few of them in most parts of England and Wales had resulted in change for the whole.

Part of the thrust to improve information for parents, inspection of schools, also got off to a reasonable start. Ofsted was established successfully and let the first round of contracts for inspecting secondary schools. As expected, most of the contracts went to groups of LEA inspectors, though there was some healthy competition from teams of private inspectors which had set themselves up around individual HMIs or LEA inspectors who had taken early retirement (and were therefore able to offer their services cheaply) as a result of the slimming down of those inspection forces. The testing was proving more problematical. The quality of the tests devised by SEAC never totally solved the conundrum of how to operate a cheap but comprehensive test. The teachers had become increasingly exercised not only by the workload which the tests required but also by the intention to use the results in league tables of schools and for performance-related pay. The result was a total boycott of the tests supported by most of the teachers' unions in 1993. The work on the publication of GCSE and A level results continued with the addition of some further information about attendance, and this was bedded in as part of the scenery. Patten was not, however, able to extend it to primary schools.

Gillian Shephard (1994–7)

Gillian Shephard began her period of office with a style which was in marked contrast to that of her immediate predecessors. She held early meetings with the teachers' unions and the LEAs and insisted that her first school visit as Secretary of State should be to an LEA rather than a grant-maintained school. She moved quickly into discussions with the National Union of Teachers about their continuing concerns on testing. She accepted without demur the final version of the National Curriculum which confirmed the non-prescriptive, teacher-led style and content recommended in the draft. She confirmed John Patten's promise of a five-year moratorium on further change. It seemed she wanted peace, with collaboration ranking as high as competition in her priorities.

This set the tone for her first year of office. There was a tacit acceptance that the grant-maintained sector would settle at just over 1000 schools (less than 5 per cent of the total), with most of them in relatively few LEA areas. She encouraged Dearing's conciliatory and minimalistic approach to the curriculum and testing. The result was a much better relationship between central and local government and the unions. LEAs were encouraged to play a full part in improving the standards of teaching and learning. She pressed ahead with plans for maintaining a four-year cycle of inspection (though there remain serious doubts about the achievability of this and the effect on the quality of the inspections being conducted) but she backed away from some of the more contentious testing programmes and softened the approach to publishing test results. All of these seemed to point to a less prominent place for the market in the education system.

During the summer of her second year of office, however, there were two strong signals of a resurgence in market philosophy. The Conservative Party think-tanks, principally the Adam Smith Institute, the Centre for Policy Studies and the Institute for Economic Affairs, were competing for attention. All of them were avid marketeers. All three had lost ground to the Civil Service in forming policy and they wanted a victory to re-establish their position. Their first was in nursery education. The Prime Minister had become convinced that an expansion of nursery education was a vote-winner and, given the disastrous standing of the government in opinion polls, was looking for popular measures. When this became known, there was a determined and organized campaign from think-tanks (with the Adam Smith Institute in the foreground) to resurrect the voucher idea and the introduction of a new programme for a non-statutory age group provided the ideal opportunity for them. At first there was an equally determined briefing from the Department for Education about the bureaucratic costs of a voucher scheme, the lowering of standards which would probably result for a particularly vulnerable age group and the question of whether vouchers would produce a market in any case. These arguments held sway for a time but the stately progress of Whitehall decision-making was knocked off course when, for internal party reasons, the Prime Minister put himself up for re-election as leader of the Conservative Party. He needed vote-winners quickly and pronounced during his re-election campaign that there was to be a nursery programme, and it was to be run on vouchers – despite the fact that mechanisms for running a nursery programme were still bogged down in Whitehall committees. A little later the Prime Minister gave a newspaper interview in which he gave some prominence to his own wish to see all schools opt out of LEA control and indicated that he would be prepared to take new measures to make sure this happened even if parents did not want it.

These statements clearly signalled the continuing strength of the market in Conservative Party thinking. The leaders of the party were convinced that education was to figure very highly in the next general election and they needed a big idea. The market was the only big idea around. It had been at the centre of their thinking for so long that there was nowhere else to go.

Meanwhile, there were important developments in Labour Party thinking. The 'New Labour' Party was looking for a big idea of its own and was anxious to see that its programme could not be construed as reverting to corporatism dominated by LEAs and teachers' unions. Its answer lay in a redefinition of the role of LEAs. They were to be facilitators, enablers, supporters of schools, not regulators. They were to make services available to those schools who were prepared to pay for them, rather than make decisions and incur costs on schools' behalf as they did before they were required to delegate decision-making and power. Grant-maintained schools would come back within this local education framework but would have the choice of whether they wished to operate as county schools (to be relabelled 'community schools'), aided schools, or a mixture of the two (to be labelled 'foundation schools'). So Labour had not totally renounced the market. A Labour government would continually emphasize school-level planning and diversity. At the same time, however, Labour believed it had found a way to reconcile these freedoms with some degree of planning and accountability to a local democracy.

Conclusion

Because this chapter has been about the market experiment, it has been written to make it seem that all the reforms described were solely directed towards producing a totally free and full market. Of course, life is not like that. No government is free to direct all its attention to a single objective, or capable of doing so even if given the power. Of the secretaries of state holding office during the period described, only Sir Keith Joseph and possibly Kenneth Clarke had a clear aim in mind; and only two or three Civil Servants understood and were committed to their vision. Governments generally stagger along reacting to events as they happen; indeed there is a little maxim which passes among Department for Education officials from time to time which says that 'all education legislation has precisely the opposite effect of that intended by those who introduced it'.

Nevertheless, there was a philosophical thread joining together the reforms of the 1980s. The market might not have been the sole or even the principal reason for the introduction of all of them. But it was there in the background affecting all these decisions to some extent. It is certainly proper to look back over that period and to ask how far those decisions have produced a market and what effect that market had on the quality of teaching and learning in our schools.

The National Curriculum did not become a contract for schools in the terms it was proposed to follow. The documents now enshrined in law give the curriculum an air of authority but the wording is so woolly that there could be no prospect of a challenge against a school which was not observing it. In any event, who would notice? LEA inspectorates are now much weakened and are less likely to pick up a maverick school than they were a decade ago. Ofsted inspection would pick up a blatant departure of a school across all subjects but there is no evidence that anyone – LEAs, parents or the government – would take any notice of major departures in some subjects. There are those who argue that the very existence of the constant changes in the documents since 1989 has kept teachers on their toes. Others claim that these changes have dulled teachers' sensitivities. Perhaps the proposed five-year moratorium on change will prove who is right.

The second pillar of the market seems reasonably intact. There is no doubt that schools are now operating more independently than they were. For LEA schools the very existence of grant-maintained status had a significant effect. LEAs now administer their schools in a much more collaborative, helpful and supportive way. They are much more school-friendly. At the same time, many LEAs stopped making hard decisions about school closures and getting into difficult questions such as whether certain head teachers should not be developing a keener interest in early retirement.

The initial wave of grant-maintained schools experienced a considerable sense of liberation on achieving their new status. Grant-maintained status gave head teachers virtually total power over their institution. Most of them were able to manipulate their governing bodies and many of the first grant-maintained schools had more money and direct access to ministers who gave them total backing. This did not, however, last long. It was soon apparent that the initial largess which they had been receiving would not last and that administrative procedures had to be put in place to monitor the expenditure of public money. Head teachers found themselves dealing with a bureaucracy similar to the one which LEAs had now become. Indeed, when the Funding Agency for Schools started to wield its planning powers it seemed possible that grant-maintained schools were being handled in a less friendly way than LEA schools. Whatever the truth of this, head teachers were treated generally with more respect and this made them happier; whether it improved their performance in leading their schools is not so certain.

In terms of meeting the third objective, the government also has seen some success. There is now a much more direct and overt relationship between the success of schools in recruiting pupils and the budgets of those schools. Delegation of resources to schools has gone far beyond the statutory requirement in many areas and the similarity between the funding system and educational vouchers is apparent. However, the linkages within schools between pupil numbers and pay is probably weaker than it was, particularly at head teacher level. There is also some indication that the general relationship between money and budgets will weaken as more and more central government revenue and capital is put into funds where schools and other public bodies are required to bid for it. The Single Regeneration Fund, Section 11, European Social Fund, National Lottery funds are all operating now on bidding systems. Some schools are succeeding in these bids and others are not, hence blurring the relationship with numbers on roll. It is often the case that the most successful bids are mounted with LEAs and other agencies as part of a collaborative programme, not as individual schools in competition.

Finally, the information systems for parents of children in secondary schools were enhanced in line with government intentions. A level and GCSE league tables are now produced in forms which are accessible to parents and the inspection programme is progressing more or less as planned. For primary schools, however, there has been less progress. A much simplified system of testing at 7 and 11 is in place, but there are continuing doubts about its value. The Ofsted inspection programme has more or less collapsed and it is becoming increasingly apparent that a four-year cycle of high-quality inspections cannot be achieved. It is becoming accepted that there needs to be a new programme for inspection which will probably look remarkably like the regime which the present system replaced.

Does this amount overall to more choice and diversity? Is there now a market system? The answer is probably 'to some extent'. There is evidence of an increase in competition between schools, but it is not the free market that was planned. The pillars on which the market-place was to be built have not proved robust enough to sustain a system radically different from the planned, consensual approach of the post-war period. The market-place stands slightly more prominently than before, but the town hall and the church are also still there standing alongside it, as important features of the civic landscape.

Whether this remains the position for long is another question that goes beyond any instant political change. Certain attitudes might harden into a further commitment to the market – to direct control by central government of all schools, the introduction of vouchers more generally and a restriction of other mechanisms for competition and payment by results. The Labour administration has essentially continued the same policies.

The great experiment may not yet be over.

Note

1 Department for Education, *Choice and Diversity* (London: HMSO, 1992).

4

Children's experience of primary schools: has it changed?

Cedric Cullingford

Children are the *raison d'être* of schools, but they are rarely central to the interests of those responsible for reforms. Their distinctive voice and their individual experiences tend to be overshadowed by the attention paid to those matters that are easier to control. Despite the principles of the Children Act, the legislation that has affected schools over the years still concentrates on the way the curriculum is delivered rather than the way it is received and on the governance of schools rather than the effects on pupils.

The amount of legislation and reform has made teachers grimly aware of constant change and constant pressure.[1] The National Curriculum and its attendant assessments and reports, league tables and the appraisal of teachers, are all examples of external reforms that have made an impact on teachers. The question remains whether the pupils in the schools have also been affected by these changes, and whether they have even noticed them. Children's experience of school is, after all, a complex matter. There are some things that never seem to change in the way schools function, and at the same time children's experiences are so varied that it is as difficult for them to detect general shifts of emphasis.

When the ways in which schools function and teaching styles are analysed it is clear that there is a great deal of variety.[2] The Oracle Report of 1980 was a major piece of research into primary education, and its findings described an almost bewildering mixture of approaches.[3] It is therefore no surprise that there should be repeated public calls to return to what is perceived as successful formality.[4] The question which is not addressed, however, is how children actually perceive these supposed differences. It could be that to them all teaching styles are 'formal' just as all questions are 'closed'.[5] It could be that what children detect in teachers are not their approaches but their expectations. If we observe the practices of the classroom we detect two facts that seem not to change. The first is the emphasis on the traditional curriculum, or what some call the 'basics'. Fifteen years ago, the Oracle Report concluded that 'the general pattern of the traditional curriculum skills prevails', bearing out the findings of the Primary Survey of 1978.[6] Little seems to have changed since then. The second is that the experience of school is centred not so much on group work, as commonly thought, but on individual work. From children's points of view they are by themselves, however they are organized. As Neville Bennett describes it: 'Groups tend to be no more than collections of children sitting together but engaged in individual work. In such groups the level of cooperation, frequency of explanations and knowledge exchange is low'.[7] The result is that for many children the actual experience of school is the repeated carrying out of familiar tasks, of practice, of hearing the teacher say 'do it again'.[8]

Schools might vary, but there is a similarity of everyday experience that children share, the simple facts of being on time, being registered, and moving from classroom to playground to assembly hall. They share a distinct view of what school is for and why they are there.[9] At the same time, there are different ways of approaching classroom work, and the experiences will vary according to the approaches. There are those who work hard and steadily, those who constantly seek attention, and those who work only intermittently.[10] And there are also the significant number of 'invisible' children who seek to remain obscure.[11] We need to bear in mind, therefore, both the variety of environments, the pupils' individual characteristics and the personalities of the teachers as well as those experiences of school which are shared by all children.

The evidence on which this chapter is based derives from research undertaken through semi-structured interviews with 160 children aged from 6 to 9. What makes this particular research different from that reported in *The Inner World of the School* is that the children talked about their experience of school in the context of their normal lives.[12] They spoke of their homes and their environment, and what they said about school arose naturally out of this. There is a commonly observed phenomenon that when children are asked what they did in school, perhaps by their parents, they answer 'Nothing' or 'I don't know'. It is as if the world of school is quite separate from that of the home, and needs to be kept separate. In these interviews the children talked naturally about their experience of school as a significant part in the pattern of their lives. They talked of the social aspects of school as well as the formal curriculum. They talked without any sense of 'closed' questions, or trying to please the interviewer. While this is not the place to elaborate on the methodology, it should be pointed out that the transcripts were all subject to content analysis to make sure that when a statement is made such as the 'children said' it means there is a consistency of experience and not a generalization from the illuminating example. As others have needed to point out, the evidence is 'hard' even if it is complex.[13] The attitudes that children express are representative of inner-city, suburban and rural backgrounds; what they have in common is not a result of a skewed sample.

For their pupils, schools are a formal social system. For most of them it is the first experience of social hierarchies and social control. School demonstrates two important social phenomena: the need for rules and the dependence on a hierarchy.[14] Children not only observe rules but also feel they are profoundly necessary. They are constrained by a whole series of practices, from standing in line to putting up their hands to gain the teacher's attention. Even the school with the most liberal intentions relies on rules for successful management. Even when children do not obey the rules they feel that they are a necessary and inevitable constraint. Even if they complain when the rules are interpreted 'unfairly' it is because the wrong child was 'picked on' rather than because of the nature of the rule itself. Children have a strong sense of the frailty and disobedience of human nature. They experience it every day. They are adamant that schools need rules, and that schools are run well only when these rules are clear. Schools are often experienced as a formal system to which children should be subservient.

Children are also strongly aware of the hierarchies within schools. This is not only a sense of the difference between teachers and themselves. They see the status of the head teacher and deputy head in relation to the others. They are also aware of the constraints on the staff from external influences, including governors.[15] Schools are first and foremost a social system in which there are clear rules and expectations, a clear agenda and an attempt to make all pupils and staff share a common purpose and a common morality. But from the point of view of the children all the rules, the hidden as well as the shared assumptions, are laid down by the teachers. Even when there are systems of 'contracts' of behaviour agreed with pupils, many children believe that these are to help the teachers, not themselves.

Children might be the *raison d'être* of schools, but they do not often see themselves like that. They see themselves as there to please the teachers, to do what the teacher wants. When they do not know what the teacher wants they try to guess it. Even in the most informal of teaching 'styles' it is the teacher who commands, who says what happens. 'Children seek to please teachers by delivering the goods teachers appear to want. Children learn what teachers want by monitoring what the reward is.'[16]

All that happens in school derives from this relationship with the teacher. Teachers' personalities might vary as much as the children's but if children believe that everything is done *for* the teacher then this has profound implications. It means that neither the purpose of school nor the relevance of the curriculum is ever explored. There are different perceptions between children and adults. As far as pupils are concerned, they enter a culture in which decision-making and choices are curtailed.[17] Children are not choosing to do things but guessing what it is that the teachers want. Teachers, whatever the style, are the focus of attention, closely observed for signs of friendliness or weakness. Children are always aware of teachers' attitudes to them.[18] Most teachers try to treat all children equally but children still detect differences, like the suppressed or hidden relief when a particularly difficult child is absent. Children detect subtle differences at one level, but also similarities at another. The teacher might feel that some lessons go much better than others; to the children it all tends to seem the same.

Teachers are observed as the begetters of both pain and pleasure. They are the ones who initiate the proceedings, who set the tasks and choose the topics. They decide who is to be rewarded and who is to be punished. All tasks that children undertake are to fulfil the teachers demands, whether they like it or not:

> I don't like writing when the teacher tells us.
>
> (Boy, 9)

> They always say 'work it out by yourself'.
>
> (Girl, 8)

Teachers are to be pleased, and the rewards appreciated.

> This term I've got the teacher's special award in assembly and quite a few gold stars and quite a few team points. It means they've done good work and they've behaved . . . I produced good work and I did good work and I never gave up doing the good working system.
>
> (Boy, 7)

Schools are symbolic of a hierarchical society. But in contrast to this, schools are also the centre of the social world of children. It is the place where they meet their friends and test friendships, where they meet enemies and are bullied. Within the formal structure of school lies an alternative and very powerful world of relationships between peers. Often the two 'cultures' clash. Pupils are all aware that there are many who not only break the rules but also appear to be either against or outside the system. It is not only those who are excluded who notice the rift, but those who observe them breaking the rules.

> There is this naughty boy. He doesn't go to school. He throws stones. And he's rudeness.
>
> (Girl, 8)

But all children are aware of 'naughtiness', in themselves as well as others. Naughtiness is closely linked with 'getting into trouble', and this is something which affects all:

> We are never always good because you have to stick up for yourself.
>
> (Girl, 9)

> My mum wants me to get away from this school really. My mum doesn't want to talk about it but she might take me away from this school. She doesn't want me to be with John. He's the one with the black hair. We get in enormous trouble.
>
> (Boy, 7)

There is therefore another important and alternative system that children experience in parallel with that of the school. This is the system of relationships; the forming of friendships and enmities, the social discovery of pupils in relation to each other. This system is the most important for many children, for it includes the pressure and influences of peers. The social system of children dominates all the areas outside the formal curriculum. It operates in the playground. It continues, under cover, in the work of classrooms. It spills over into life away from school. Many of the real tensions and difficulties, as well as the pleasures of school, arise from this system of relationships.

The formal and informal social systems associated with school overlap. This can provide tensions. It is possible to trace the development of truants to the way in which one system – formal schooling – is rendered powerless in the face of the other – the pressure of peers and the forming of groups. The ways in which children 'test' the formal system in their relationships with teachers shows how powerful and influential is the alternative system, and shows how aware all children are of their own culture as well as that of the school.

For children the network of relationships outside as well as within the classroom is an extremely important part of school, and for some the most important. When they describe the experience of school it is the social factors on which they concentrate; on the emotional effects of relationships made the more complex by the competitiveness of which they are all aware. There are, in fact, two overlapping themes that keep emerging from their descriptions of school life – intense relationships, including bullying, and self-conscious awareness of their own work performance in relation to others.

There is a constant juxtaposition in the experience of school between the demands of the classroom and the pressures of relationships. When children explore their experience they are far more concerned with the latter than the former, even when they talk about the curriculum. This is because of the intense need for friends, to be liked at least by some people. One great fear is to have no friends.

Anyhow I haven't got that much friends. I don't know. I got no friends except for David. That's only one friend. I wish I was different.

(Boy, 8)

People leave me out of games and they don't really play with me much . . . There's a new girl and, well Mrs B told me to go out and play with her, well Nikki came up and pushing me out of the way.

(Girl, 8)

Schools are places where children test social relationships, often changing allegiances.[19] While there are distinctions to be made between those who are nearly always lonely or ostracized and those only occasionally so, from time to time most children experience the pain of being rejected by their peers. Children's attitudes towards their own abilities, and therefore their motivation to work, are affected by their relationships. The security or insecurity of school is dependent on their feeling that they have friends of like mind, that there are people to play and to work with. Partnerships are as important in the classroom as in the playground.

Children suffer when relationships go wrong, or when they cannot sustain them. It is then that they are at their most vulnerable, when they are most likely to be 'picked on'. Children not only observe bullying but are threatened by it. It is frequently mentioned as part of the everyday life of school. Like 'getting into trouble', children find themselves personally caught up in it. It is for some a developing mixture of reactions to other people and personal initiatives. The justification is 'sticking up for yourself' in the face of other people's physical or verbal attacks. But it can be very hard to see the distinction between provocation and defence. What is clear is that physical violence often becomes a form of life within the social ambience of the school.

Some people don't like me probably because, like, if they start kicking me and that I just get hold of them and throw them across the playground or something because I get annoyed. If only people wouldn't come up to me and start kicking me and that. When they start if I can catch them I just get up and swing them round me and make them go spinning round because I get so annoyed with them. They do it to some other people and call them names. Well, really horrible names. The one that does it to me is younger than me but I'm taller than him. Sometimes I just walk away but he comes back at you and that until, like, you just get hold of him and just throw him across the playground kind of. He just kind of smiles and then because he knows that I don't like swearing . . . I don't do it back and that's why he can get me back. I just try to forget about it and the next day, sometimes he comes back on it and that. My dad told me something to say to him and he said 'I don't care' which was a bit naughty.

(Boy, 8)

The mixture of frustration, anger and provocation are all finely balanced. Out of a sense of isolation, of not being liked, comes the violent response. The very fact that the child is so easily provoked makes him a clearer target. The concept of 'protecting yourself' is seen as necessary against those who either form groups, or are stronger, or both. The tendency to hit back, to be provoked, itself singles out children as victims as well as bullies.

Children see bullies as an inevitable if regrettable fact of school life, as if they were the pathological end of testing relationships. Bullying is not just physical, which is why it is so closely linked to other experiences. Being 'picked on' or teased can hurt as much as anything. Being ignored or ostracized has deep effects. The reasons given for being singled out as a victim are nearly always concerned with being 'different'.[20] This can be for a variety of reasons, but applies to anyone who stands out from the others, whether for physical or mental reasons:

> That I've got curly hair and stuff. Its not my fault that my hair sticks up, is it? Because they're all white here and there's no browns. And they think that my clothes are funny but they're just the same as theirs.
>
> (Girl, 7)

Children sense that there are a series of different cultural systems, and a lack of conformity to that of the majority is a cause of tension. This does not mean that the behaviour is justified. Indeed, children understand the complexity of relationships, the reasons for bad behaviour, the pain of the victim as well as the frustration of the perpetrator. There is no simple distinction to be made between the 'bad' bully and the innocent victim. The struggle for self-identity in relation to others is difficult and complex. Take this example of insight into different points of view; a mixture of personal pain and of understanding:

> People leave me out of games and they don't really play with me much. Like today . . . and, well, Nabila came up and she wasn't treating me very well in the game and pushing me out of the way.
> She's been through a rough patch. Nearly everyone keeps on saying that she's, um, that she looks like the colour of poo, just because she's black. Since then, whenever somebody's not nice to her or they don't want to do things she always gets a bit frustrated and angry and takes it out on everyone. And she thinks they actually try to say to her that they don't like her because she's black. But that isn't always true.
> It wasn't just Nabila in the game. It was everybody else. She didn't make me very happy and when I said I'm not playing they all said 'Good'. And even Catherine said it. And well, when I'd gone off Nabila was gone off as well. She was crying. And so was I. And then

I went over and Catherine came to me and said 'What's the matter?' and I said 'I'm just not playing. I'm fed up'. And Catherine just went off. And Nabila came up to her and she's just taken over Catherine now. Catherine does not like me any more.

I've got plenty of other friends.

I feel a bit sorry for her 'cos sometimes when I say I like her she doesn't believe me. Like, well, when everyone is being horrible to her she says 'No one likes me. I haven't got any friends'. And I say 'I like you, Nabila. You're my friend'. And she just walks off in a huff and says 'You're just pretending. I know you don't like me because I'm black'. People, they say that to her so maybe she feels that no one likes her at all. Because one person started it off saying she was black 'cos she's the colour of poo. 'Cos they just want to cause trouble and be spiteful. Some children have been through a rough patch themselves, so they take it out on other children. It makes them go through a rough patch just because they've gone through a rough patch at home.

(Girl, 8)

The tensions between children derive from their strong desire to be liked – just as they want to be loved by parents – and the realization that there are temptations to be nasty that are difficult to resist, as in sibling rivalry. Which way children will turn depends so much on the subtle influence of the peer group. They both *understand* what it is like to be victimized and find the pleasure of joining in almost irresistible. For most children this tension is controlled; one is balanced by the other. For a few children the sense of isolation from others is not overcome – whether this comes about for superficial reasons such as physical appearance, or deeper traumas that derive from the home. What is clear is that once set in a certain direction it is easy for all kinds of factors to reinforce it.

The realization that children share is that 'difference' means being marked for attention. This difference does not have to be a weakness. On the contrary, it can be the very fact that there is someone better, cleverer or prettier than the others.

Whoever's the best in the class is usually bossiest and everyone doesn't like you very much because they're jealous of you being the best. And they think you're bossy, like Eve. She used to be in our class and she was the best at everything. And she had loads of boyfriends and everyone hated her because she, she didn't really care. She was mean to everyone. Bossy, unfair and cruel and well, everyone thought that she was the prettiest in the class and they were so jealous of her, really. So they were all being horrible to her but she didn't care. She's left and now she's gone off to travel round the world.

(Girl, 8)

As we will see, competition is very important to children. They would like to be among the best without standing out. When someone is the best in every way and does not mind standing out, that is a cause for jealousy. But it is also a sign of invulnerability, and the majority of children who fear becoming victims do so either because they fear being teased for defects, or physically attacked because of weakness.

> I wish I could go to school and nobody's going to beat me up and things.
>
> (Boy, 8)

> I don't like to be small because some people can like pick on me which I don't like it very much.
>
> (Boy, 8)

The fear of being physically or mentally hurt is a pervasive one. It appears in all kinds of statements in all kinds of contexts. It has been noted that this is an *accepted* part of the social culture of school. This does not imply that it is acceptable, or taken for granted by children. Physical attacks are the most visible sign of what makes children anxious. Their trepidation in the world is a lack of confidence that they will be safe, at school, in the street or even in the home.

For children schools contain both formal and informal systems, and there are both connections and conflicts between them. It is well established that underlying any academic success is the ability to make relationships, to understand social habits and to create certain kinds of dialogue.[21] The security, or lack of it, that children feel both with each other and with the demands of the teacher is an important factor. Every experience in school provides the opportunity for a variety of relationships. Schools highlight those who are misfits and those who go against the collective ethos – of the teachers or the pupils. Not fitting into one set of values puts pressure on children to fit into another. If the ethos of the school – working hard, obeying the rules and pleasing the teacher – is rejected it is usually for the sake of alternative style, with its other types of conformity. But for virtually all children of primary school age school is a matter of balancing one system against the other. Both are important: 'fitting in' and 'not standing out'.

Nowhere is the tension between formal and informal systems better seen than in children's attitudes to their own work in relation to that of others. It is in academic work that children's views of themselves against both formal and informal standards emerges. Their attitudes towards the curriculum show that they are aware of what subjects consist of, and their status in a hierarchy of importance, at the same time as picking out significant lessons or topics that stand out against the everyday. The emphasis on maths and writing makes their dominant status quite clear.[22] They are also aware of subject such as history, even when they do not take them under that heading.[23] But what they remember comes across as far more arbitrary.

> We are talking about different countries and the most countries we were talking about were Germany and India. But this year we're talk-ing about chocolate.
>
> (Boy, 8)

> We did something about the Celts. And we're doing about France.
>
> (Girl, 8)

Topics are undergone or 'done' and change from term to term. It might be part of the 'don't know' syndrome, but there is no hint of any sense of pur-pose or reason in doing them. Instead certain teachers are associated with particular enthusiasms;

> But in Mr N when you get to his class you will talk about Germany. Because they do science and about countries.
>
> (Girl, 6)

> When I was in Mrs C's class we all dressed up and we did dancing and we had funny sort of clothes on.
>
> (Girl, 9)

> At my old school in the last class when I had just become eight my teacher was interested in green things.
>
> (Boy, 9)

Children rarely mention the curriculum with great enthusiasm. Particular lessons or interests might stand out but the diurnal experience is much more mundane. Routine lessons with repeated exercises like arithmetic or writing are commonplace, with some of the more able children especially fulfilling tasks for which they have already demonstrated their capacity.[24] Even doing too well, or finishing a task too quickly or successfully, is seen as something to be avoided:

> Sometimes when I do my work quickly I'm really bored afterwards. And so if you finish slowly you won't be bored.
>
> (Girl, 8)

There are particular kinds of demands that teachers make, like neatness:

> Otherwise I get told to do it again or something.
>
> (Boy, 8)

> Everyone might have done it too quickly and made it not very neat and if I spent a long time doing it it might come out neater than the

others. My teacher makes me practise instead of getting on with my other work.

(Boy, 8)

What emerges from children's description of their experience of school is not the enthusiasm for the good moments as much as the fear of failure. The curriculum is not so much a series of exciting topics as a competition in which there are winners and losers. The competition is not just against the teachers' expectations but against each other, but it is a more subtle competition than the desire to be the best. Children are, like their parents, both aware of and curious about their own performance in relation to their peers.[25] By the age of 8 they are aware that hard work and academic success are not closely related.[26] This can cause significant traumas.

Whatever standards a school sets the sense that children have is that they do not meet them, that there are always more difficult things to strive towards, things they cannot do or easily understand. Children get frustrated at their own lack of ability.

I'm not a fast learner and everything I learn sometimes it goes out of my head.

(Boy, 8)

I feel I haven't learned much. They've got stuff right and I've got them wrong and feel that I've not learned much and I haven't been paying attention.

(Girl, 8)

I'm getting really frustrated with my work. I'm very slow at doing things.

(Boy, 8)

If they've got difficulties and they get more right than you I feel ashamed. 'Cos they say if you don't finish it you've got to stay in and do it. And if the person that's not as good as you does it before you, you feel sort of not very good.

(Girl, 8)

There are two powerful strands of experience. One is the lack of self-worth, a disbelief in, or frustration with, their own lack of ability. The other is the finely tuned sensitivity to the performance of other children, in terms of their ability and their success. The competition of school is not a simple one of striving to be best, not a league table of success, but a sense of making the best use of the talents available. It is being 'beaten' by others who do not have the same ability that is galling. Their own limitations are placed in the context of other children.

When I mean I'm not very good at writing I mean I'm not very good at spelling. 'Cos I try to do words and I get a few right but not as much as I get wrong. I mean I get more wrong that I do right. I'm worse than some of them and better than others.

(Boy, 8)

When I do something wrong I have to write it out again and again. Sometimes it's a bit hard 'cos sometimes I don't know how to say something. And its a bit hard to write it down for me. Sometimes I want to be able to finish it off. If I don't finish it people think that I don't know much things about them.

(Girl, 8)

I look at other people and they've done it much better.

(Boy, 8)

One of the crucial factors for children in the classroom is the relationship between the speed of doing the work and its neatness. They are aware of two conflicting pressures – to make sure that they get the work done in the allotted time and to do it well enough so that it does not have to be repeated. Neatness of presentation takes time, and this can mean that they are holding up the others. They do not want to hold up the class or to be singled out for the teacher's attention. To get the task done is one issue; to 'keep up' is another. The competition is not just about a successful end-product but about speed.

I like doing my work neatly and they do it not very neatly. I do feel terrible when I'm not the best at something because I always go last. Terrible because I would never get my work done.

(Boy, 6)

The reason I'm last is because I'm slow because I take it nice and calmly but all the other ones are so good at it. They do it really fast and its good. But I don't. 'Cos I'm not very good at stuff.

(Girl, 8)

When I've just been off school and I'm better and I come back and they've gone ahead of me. I try to work as quick as I can. Well, I just mainly try to keep up.

(Boy, 8)

I have to learn everything so quickly to get with them. I've got to do that and like that because they've done plus and minus and all of those.

(Girl, 8)

There is a constant pressure on the children to keep up, or catch up, a sense of urgency which derives not just from the teacher who is the final judge of success or failure, but from each other. They judge their own work not against set criteria or against attainment targets but in competition with each other. They are conscious of a race. They do not wish to be exposed as slow, and be embarrassed.

> They just might be a bit cleverer than me. And they're getting things quicker than me. Once I did my sums, one of my sums quickly and then another person started going really quickly so that I had to catch up with them. And it was a race. When we were running to the teacher and trying to show her . . . Sometimes they say I'm slow at things and that I'm not clever or anything.
>
> (Girl, 8)

> My best friend, he might have done it before me and I think I'm going to be really embarrassed.
>
> (Boy, 8)

The sense of individual work done in competition against others is pervasive and supports the research that has been carried out on the lack of success of most group work.[27] Even if the teacher sets tasks that are designed for cooperative learning the children tend to concentrate on what they do by themselves.

> Sometimes when you're doing maths things you have to do it quietly, sit on your own, with books around you so that no one will copy you or you can't copy them. I start sweating and feel 'Oh, I'm not going to be able to do this, and everyone's going to finish before me' and things like that.
>
> (Girl, 8)

There is a significant pressure on the children not to finish last. Once they cease to care about this they are no longer part of the formal 'system'. While at primary school, and certainly around the age of 8, they take this pressure very seriously. It might not matter any more for those who begin to feel excluded from the system because of their lack of success, but it does at an age when they still feel the pain of not keeping up. This sense of competition is driven much more by the desire not to be the worst than the desire to be the best. In fact there are inhibitions about doing too well, for anyone who stands out is seen as 'different'. Doing very well is likened to 'showing off'.

> I'd like to be at a stage where you're not someone who needs help but someone whose not brainy, but not having difficulties.
>
> (Girl, 8)

> I don't really mind if I'm not first, but I don't really mind if I'm last, but I hope I'm *nearer* the first one.
>
> (Boy, 8)

It's just that I feel as though that I'm the least cleverest in the whole class. It's not that I want to be the cleverest, it's just that I want to get on with my spelling and work.

(Girl, 8)

Sad, because they think like 'We're the best'. They say like 'I know more things than you' and stuff like that.

(Boy, 8)

I don't really care when people show off when they are ahead.

(Boy, 7)

Just as it is sensible to do work slowly to guard against boredom, so there is social pressure not to 'show off', not to be too outstanding, not to be too different. The attractions of the average, of the norm, are as strong in the academic as in the social aspects of school. This does not prevent children being aware of their own abilities. They know that success and failure lie in their own hands.[28] But they also are increasingly aware of the distinctions between ability and achievement. As they get older so the ratings of their own abilities decline – a self-fulfilling prophecy.[29] They are also aware of many social, non-academic influences on their performance in school. They find that there are times when competition is unfair, either because of lack of teacher attention or distractions.

It's quite hard and that and the teacher's helping somebody else. Like helping another person who gets there before me and I get a bit annoyed about that as well.

(Boy, 8)

Some people like whisper to me and that and I just whisper back and they keep on doing it. And I just keep on doing it. I don't get my work done. Sometimes she says 'That's not a lot, is it?' and things like that.

(Boy, 8)

The sense of competition in getting tasks done, in keeping up, is paralleled by their judgements of their own and others' abilities. They do not want to let down their families.

It worries me because my mum and dad they're quite clever and my brother's quite clever, so I'd think I'm not the same. I don't like to be the smallest unclever. I know its a bit boring but it's important to learn things. I know it's very boring sometimes.

(Boy, 8)

The experience of school is intense, and not always happy. It is both individual at times, with moments of isolation, and very social at other times. The significance of the intensity of school lies in the mass of complex relationships. Friendships are being tested. New groups are being formed. Admiration for some is mixed with quarrels with others. School, in fact, provides for intense emotional life through competitiveness and working with friends and being distracted by others from the formal curriculum. There are all kinds of relationships taking place and judgements being made.

He's not a very nice boy because he used to be not very nice to me in the infants. But actually now when we're in the juniors he's been quite nice to me. I've been playing with him.

Sometimes I push people over by accident and they say I did it on purpose so I get annoyed. And sometimes I get in trouble and I say 'That's not fair!' and things like that. And I think I shouldn't do that but I can't stop myself 'cos they push me over as well sometimes. But I still don't swear.

Sometimes this girl at school called Beth, she's nasty but sometimes she's nice. So I can't make up my mind. She sucks her fingers and her friend called Kirsty, they're really good friends because they've known each other since they were in nursery and they both suck their fingers and thumbs. Sometimes they don't let me play with them so I don't. And then later on she says 'Do you want to play with me?' so I say 'Oh, all right'.

If they were first – all the people were first – and I was last I would have to stay in when it's home time and I would actually like to go home. It's just that they're better than me and some day I'll learn more than them. I wouldn't be good at a lot of things and I wouldn't be able to move to seniors very quick and I'd be the last person and things like that. There's um two boys I know they are very good at writing, spelling. One's called Martin and he's a very good runner and things like that as well and he knows virtually about everything.

(Girl, 7)

Here we see many of the threads of school life woven together. Judgements are made of character and ability. Relationships are volatile and friendships easily made and dropped. There is violence and accusation. There are temperamental changes, with insiders and outsiders. There is self-consciousness and worry as well as pleasure and appreciation.

Children's essential experience of school is a very personal one, but also one which is widely shared. Despite different styles of teaching and a changing curriculum, there are certain fundamental experiences that make any reforms appear comparatively superficial. Children are all exposed to formal social structure within which there are many alternative social relationships. They all respond to the paramount importance of the teacher's wishes but they do so with a sharp awareness of the importance of each other. The desire not to stand out, to avoid ridicule or victimization is as true inside the classroom as in the playground. The nature of schooling does not suddenly change.

And yet there have been subtle changes in the experience of schooling since the early 1980s, before the 1988 Education (Reform) Act. Given the slow nature of change, one might have expected a shift in emphasis due to the developments since the Plowden Report – the argument about the nature of the curriculum, the balance between the autonomy of the learner and the control of the teacher, the increasing involvement of parents and ancillaries, the integration of children with special educational needs and the greater sophistication of teacher education. But all these matters, before the 1988 Act, are not detectable in the accounts given by children. The experiences on which they report are not changed by all the public arguments and debates, the political uses of parents and the attacks on teachers. Children are aware that teachers are not rated highly by politicians and in the mass media but it does not undermine the authority of their own.

But the real reforms have only been comparatively recently introduced. The question is what difference these might make to the experience and achievement of children. Will local management of schools, assessment, appraisal, league tables, parental choice which entails moving house, class size, formal teaching methods and all the manifestations of market forces be noticed by the children, let alone affect them? Any effect will, of course, be as subtle as a change in the ethos of the school, changing because of the teachers' sense of being beleaguered, distracted by external demands. But changes of this kind are slow, and depend on the particular school, in which the pupils cannot make comparisons, so they take their personal experience as being the standard one, shared to an extent by all schools.

It is worth reminding ourselves what children like and appreciate about schools and whether the reforms enhance or detract from these factors that support pupil motivation. The first essential in any classroom is that the teacher is able to 'explain'. This implies a degree of individual attention as well as clarity that means the teacher can respond to need.[30] The larger the size of the class, the more difficult this is. But explanation, that essential gift of the good teacher, is what children most urgently seek.[31] Allied to this, if less important, is the desire for good cooperative working relationships with each other, being given tasks which are not competitive but shared. Even when this does not take place, children request it as a desirable mode of learning.[32] Children wish to work together constructively, not merely sit with their friends. Again, like sustained conversations with adults, this seems comparatively rare.[33]

Children also desire confidence in their own work, which implies less constant assessment, whether formal or informal. The fact that they are constantly making comparisons and are in constant competition does not enhance the standards of their work. Instead, they long to explore something in depth, for its own sake as well as for its relevance to their understanding. The curriculum as presented to them is for the most part the domain of the teacher, a routine that has to be undergone. While children are aware of other powerful forces that control the teacher, like the National Curriculum, they still accept the teacher as the source of knowledge and control.

Children are aware of what they look for in good teaching. It could be argued that what children actually like might not be good for them. To what extent does unhappiness in school relate to achievement? Satisfaction with school is not necessarily associated with good examination results.[34] When the overall concern is with 'raising standards', should the voices of the children be taken into account? Does it signify that half of the pupils report being bored and that their motivation and positive attitudes diminish as they get older?[35]

We have argued that schools are too complex to be suddenly changed by reforms of the curriculum or of the management and appraisal of teachers. They go on performing better or worse despite rather than because of outside interference. All successful change is incremental, arising from the sense of personal ownership of the reforms, with teachers included and supported.[36] In that light the changes following the Education (Reform) Act are most likely slowly to damage the achievement of children. All the demands not only go against the hopes and expectations of children but also have been proved not to work. Those very matters which bring out the worst in pupils are being fostered: competition, a distancing of teachers and the insecurity of not being in the 'right' school. It is clear that children's abilities are not helped by tests.[37] It is also clear that the tighter the curriculum guidelines, the less teachers and pupils can work together for real individual understanding.[38] Teachers are, in the eyes of perceptive pupils, becoming deskilled. The focus of tasks and activities can mean a concentration on routines with no room for intuition or intellectual discovery. Above all, the teachers, important as they are in the eyes of their pupils, will change their professional status. Instead of having the desire and ability to extend their role, concerned with the whole of the children's education, they will become more restricted 'deliverers of the curriculum'.[39]

The possibility, then, is that over the next few years primary schools will change their nature and that the experience of pupils will reflect this change. But children are not only affected by their experience of school. There are more profound forces at work. The Children Act symbolizes a gathering realization of some of the traumas of childhood, including abuse and access to disturbing information. Notions of the helpless innocence of optimistic childhood seem hopelessly old-fashioned. The real changes that affect children are the changes in society, a sense of competitiveness and anxiety that affects them as much at home as at school. The pupils who come to school to experience the traumatic aspects of relationships and the disabling effects of competition, come with previous experience of both, living in a society in which they are much publicized. The anxiety that they experience at school as part of the 'natural' order of things continues the anxiety that they bring with them. Perhaps schools will always reflect the attitudes of the society in which they are placed; they are certainly a product of society. But it must be admitted that what children so clearly articulate would lead to a set of different experiences and a school system which could make greater differences. There are some signs that children are being given a voice. But those who listen to them are not being listened to by those who have the power to act.

Notes

1 Parents are also aware of this. See C. Cullingford, 'Parents' perception of the education system' in C. Cullingford, *Parents, Education and the State* (Aldershot: Arena, 1996).

2 P. Mortimore, P. Sammons, L. Stoll, D. Lewis and R. Ecob, *School Matters: The Junior Years* (Wells: Open Books, 1988).

3 M. Galton, B. Simon and P. Croll, *Inside the Primary Classroom* (London: Routledge & Kegan Paul, 1980).

4 S.N. Bennett, *Teaching Styles and Pupil Progress* (London: Open Books, 1976).

5 C. Cullingford, *The Inner World of the School* (London: Cassell, 1991); C. Cullingford, *The Effective Teacher* (London: Cassell, 1995).

6 Galton *et al.*, *Inside the Primary Classroom*, p. 155; Department of Education and Science, *Primary Education in England: A Survey by HM Inspectors of Schools* (London: HMSO, 1978).

7 S.N. Bennett, 'Cooperative learning in classrooms: processes and outcomes', *Journal of Child Psychology and Psychiatry*, 32(4), 581–94 (1991), p. 590.

8 S.N. Bennett, C. Desforges, A. Cockburn and B. Wilkinson, *The Quality of Pupil Learning Experiences* (Hove: Lawrence Erlbaum, 1984).

9 Cullingford, *The Inner World of the School*, Chapter 10.

10 M. Galton and J. Williamson, *Group Work in the Primary Classroom* (London: Routledge, 1992); A. Sluckin, *Growing Up in the Playground* (London: Routledge & Kegan Paul, 1982).

11 J. Pye, *Invisible Children: Who Are the Real Losers at School?* (Oxford: Oxford University Press, 1989).

12 This is not to suggest that there is any inconsistency in the findings. On the contrary, the messages are consistently reinforced.

13 J. Dunn, *The Beginnings of Social Understanding* (Oxford; Basil Blackwell, 1988).

14 Cullingford, *The Inner World of the School*, op cit.

15 Ibid.

16 Bennett *et al.*, *The Quality of Pupil Learning Experiences*, p. 211.

17 G. Barrett (ed.), *Disaffection from School? The Early Years* (London: Falmer Press, 1989).

18 J. Getzels and J. Smilansky, 'Individual differences in pupil perceptions of school problems', *British Journal of Educational Psychology*, 53(3), 307–16 (1983); H. Giles and M. Smith, 'Accommodation theory: optimal levels of convergence' in H. Giles and R. St Clair, *Language and Social Psychology* (Oxford: Basil Blackwell, 1979), pp. 45–65.

19 B. Davies, *Life in the Classroom and Playground: The Accounts of Primary School Children* (London: Routledge & Kegan Paul, 1982).

20 C. Cullingford and G. Brown, 'Children's perceptions of victims and bullies', *Education 3–13*, 23(2), 11–17 (1995).

21 G. Wells, *Language Development in the Pre-school Years* (Cambridge: Cambridge University Press, 1985); C. Cullingford, *The Nature of Learning* (London: Cassell, 1990).

22 H. Burgess, 'The primary curriculum: the example of mathematics' in C. Cullingford, *The Primary Teacher* (London: Cassell, 1989), pp. 16–36.

23 R. King, *The Best of Primary Education? A Sociological Study of Junior Middle Schools* (London: Falmer Press, 1989).

24 Bennett *et al.*, *The Quality of Pupil Learning Experiences*.

25 Cullingford, *Parents, Education and the State*, Chapter 4.

26 J. Eshel and J. Kurman, 'Academic self-concept, accuracy of perceived ability and academic achievements', *British Journal of Education Psychology*, 61(2), 187–96 (1991); D. Stipek and D. MacIver, 'Developmental change in children's assessment of intellectual competence', *Child Development*, 60(3), 521–38 (1989).

27 Bennett *et al.*, *The Quality of Pupil Learning Experiences*.

28 P. Blatchford, 'Children's attitude to work at 11 years', *Educational Studies*, 18(1), 107–18 (1992).

29 D. Stipek, 'Children's perceptions of their own and their classmates' ability', *Journal of Educational Psychology*, 73(3), 404–10 (1983).

30 P. Blatchford, J. Burke, C. Farquahar, I. Plewis and B. Tizard, 'A systematic observation study of children's behaviour at infant school', *Research Papers in Education*, 2(1), 47–62 (1987).

31 J. Goodnow and A. Burns, *Home and School: A Child's Eye View* (London: Allen & Unwin, 1985).

32 Blatchford *et al.*, 'A systematic observation study'.

33 S. Meadows and A. Cashdan, *Helping Children Learn: Contributions to a Cognitive Curriculum* (London: David Fulton, 1988).

34 J. Ainley and S. Bourke, 'Student views of primary schooling', *Research Papers in Education*, 7(2), 107–28 (1992).

35 W. Keys and C. Fernandes, *What Do Students Think about School?* (Slough: National Foundation for Educational Research, 1993).

36 P. Dalin, T. Ayono, A. Biazen, D. Dibowa, M. Jalian, B. Matthew, M. Rojas and C. Rojacs, *How Schools Improve. An International Report* (London: Cassell, 1994).

37 J. Nicholls and S. Hazzard, *Education as Adventure: Lessons from the Second Grade* (New York: Teachers College Press, 1993).

38 C. Bereiter and M. Scardamalia, *Surpassing Ourselves: An Enquiry into the Nature and Implications of Expertise* (Evanston, Ill.: Open Court Publishing, 1993).

39 P. Broadfoot and M. Osborn, with M. Gilly and A. Paillet, 'Teachers' conceptions of their professional responsibility: some international comparisons', *Comparative Education*, 23(3), 287–302 (1987).

5

The uses and abuses of assessment

Mary Jane Drummond

At a meeting of the Primary Education Study Group in November 1987, Professor Martin Shipman said: 'There is a close and necessary relationship between what we choose to assess and what we value most in the education of our pupils.' I wrote his words in my notebook there and then, but it has taken me a long time to understand fully what they mean for teachers in primary education today. When Shipman spoke, remember, all we knew of what was to come was in the thin red booklet, *The National Curriculum 5–16*, which appeared in the summer of 1987. We knew that attainment targets would be set for the three core subjects of maths, English and science, and that there were to be nationally prescribed tests 'to supplement the individual teachers' assessments'.[1] And we knew that an expert Task Group on Assessment and Testing (TGAT) was soon to be set up, but not much more. The concepts of choice and value, and the quality of the relationship between them, had not then been challenged by the statutory programme of assessment that was to follow in the wake of the 1988 Education (Reform) Act.

Even at the time, however, it was clear to me that this view of assessment was a principled aspiration to things as they might be rather than a full description of things as they were. For example, if the relationship between values and assessment was as close as Shipman claimed, why had I seen so many schedules for assessing children at the start of their schooling that recorded their knowledge of the names of the colours? One such schedule requires the teacher to test the child's knowledge of 12 different colours. Are the colour names really included in 'what we value most in the education of our pupils'? I could not, and cannot, believe it.

Another example: at around the same time, a colleague sent me a copy of an early screening instrument beguilingly entitled 'TEDDS', which had been developed in a local school. This format (the Two Term Early Detection of Difficulties Screen) was to be used to assess children in their second term of school on a whole range of measures, including their play. The criteria for this part of the assessment were as follows:

(P1)   Child engages in sequence of make believe actions, e.g. undresses doll, washes doll in bath, brushes hair

(P2)   Child cooperates with other children in game involving simple rules, e.g. Snap, hide and seek

(P3)   Child spends 5 minutes completing play activity, e.g. finishes 10 piece jigsaw/builds Lego house without prompting

The pinnacle of achievement suggested here, the ability to complete a ten-piece jigsaw or a Lego house, is hardly evidence of what early years educators value most in young children's play. It may be evidence that is easy to observe and record, but it can make no serious claims to educational importance.

These examples, and many others like them, some of which I have described elsewhere,[2] suggest that, back in 1987, there was at the very least a gap, if not a yawning chasm, between principle and practice, between value and performance, between the fine words spoken at educational study groups and everyday classroom life. In this chapter I will argue that the concepts of choice and value are essential to the effective assessment of children's learning and that 'the close and necessary relationship between them' must be embedded in practice, however many difficulties stand in the way. The forms of statutory assessment that have been imposed on primary teachers have already done considerable damage: I will argue that this damage can only be limited in the future if we take account of the lessons to be learned from these new forms of statutory assessment, which will, whatever we do, cast a long shadow over the independent practice of worthwhile teacher assessment.

It would be impossible in this short piece to analyse in full the inadequacies of the statutory requirements of recent years. In any case, there are other texts to turn to. In particular, Blenkin and Kelly have comprehensively reviewed the ways in which the National Curriculum testing programme is inconsistent with its stated aim of raising educational standards.[3] Here I will simply describe a few of the characteristics of this statutory testing programme that are likely to make it difficult for primary teachers to realize Shipman's precept, and to make choices that are consistent with their most strongly held educational values.

The detailed study by Gipps *et al.*[4] shows that the report of the TGAT[5] was generally welcomed by teachers, because of its emphasis on *formative teacher assessment*. This feel-good factor may have masked the anxiety

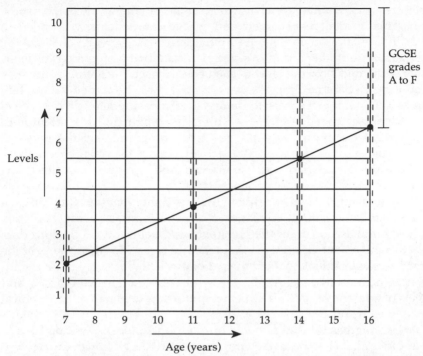

Figure 5.1 Sequence of pupil achievement of levels between ages 7 and 16

Source: Department of Education and Science, *National Curriculum Task Group on Assessment and Testing: A Report* (London: HMSO, 1988), para. 102.

triggered by another element of the report, the straight-line graph (Fig. 5.1) which represents the progression of the pupil population aged 7 to 16 from level 2 to level 6½. Especially worrying to early years educators, because of its implicit suggestion that children's educational achievements begin at the age of 7, it is even more worrying in what it suggests about learning.

This straight-line representation does damage to primary teachers by flying in the face of what we know about children's learning; that it is irregular, untidy, spasmodic, provisional and exploratory. Here, learning is represented as an evenly paced progression through hierarchically organized and predefined levels. These contrasting views of how children learn correspond, naturally enough, with different approaches to teaching. The continuing debate over the teaching of reading, for example, may seem to centre on facts and figures, on standards and specifics; but, beneath the surface, the contest is between two mutually exclusive views of teaching and learning.[6]

The uncompromising crispness of the TGAT straight line could have been seen as a warning of what was to come. As the whole cumbersome apparatus of attainment targets and profile components was unveiled, and, in preparation for the 1991 Standard Assessment Tasks (SATs), teachers were initiated into the complex calculations required to determine each child's overall level in each core subject, the nature of the new requirements became clear. Assessment was now to be carried out in a language unfamiliar to teachers: the language of measurement, precise, objective, depersonalized. Kelly saw this new language, this attempt to standardize our terms, as a process that, in suppressing the personal dimension of education, would 'take away what is the essence not only of the concept of education to which many people subscribe, but also of the reality of the educational experience for all'.[7]

Kelly was not alone in identifying the possibility that statutory forms of assessment might infect formative teacher assessment with their misguided emphasis on accuracy, specificity and neutrality. In the introduction to a passionate defence of what teachers can do for themselves in the practice of assessment, without the aid of the National Curriculum assessment structures, Michael Armstrong wrote: 'The language of targets and levels of attainment reduces achievement to a false hierarchy of technical accomplishments'.[8]

Armstrong bases his arguments on one short piece of writing by a 6-year-old girl, taken from the first report of the National Curriculum English Working Group.[9] He reproduces the official description, by the English Working Group, of the child's work, which is said to 'illustrate several Level 2 features of writing', and makes hay with their meagre account, which catalogues the writer's ways with capital letters, full stops and spelling. But there is, argues Armstrong, 'another way of looking'.

The child's story, for all its formal imperfections, so scrupulously noted by the English Working Group (for example, 'individual spellings are wrong e.g. trooth, eny, owt, sumthing, cubad'), reveals to Armstrong's way of looking, 'a young child's thought in all its imaginative richness'.[10] What is important for my argument, however, is not the richness of what Armstrong sees in this child's story, but the richness of the language in which he communicates what he sees. Armstrong is not just defending the rights of teachers to interpret, to respond to meaning, to appreciate moral conflict and drama in children's writing; he is also, equally fiercely, attacking the attempt by the National Curriculum Council to reduce the language of assessment to its bare necessities, exemplified here in a disengaged audit of spelling and handwriting.

Armstrong is making a claim for a different language for the practice of assessment – a language of critical scrutiny and appreciation. He demands a language in which teachers can describe the 'patterns of intention' in children's work: the 'interests, motifs, orientation, forms of meditation that govern a child's thought and seek expression in her practice'.[11]

In Armstrong's approach to assessment we can see clearly, in full working order, the close and necessary relationship between choice and value that, I maintain, characterizes worthwhile assessment. What Armstrong shows us is that the kind of language in which we record our assessments is one of the principled choices we have to make; we can choose the rigid neutrality of the English Working Group, or, as he does, a rich and respectful language that does justice to children's intellectual, moral and emotional powers.

The statutory assessment requirements of the National Curriculum, particularly the 1991 Key Stage 1 SATs, were experienced by primary teachers with the shock of the new. Even Gipps *et al.*, in a text characterized by the cool neutrality of a research report, describe the 1991 SATs as 'a traumatic experience'.[12] But for all their newness, these tasks, and the pencil and paper tests that superseded them in later years, were, in some important ways, a natural development of much that had gone before. The Report of the House of Commons Education, Science and Arts Committee, *Achievement in Primary Schools*,[13] for example, was notable for an emphasis on achievement that has had, I believe, some long-term effects on approaches to assessment. By focusing on the concept of *achievement*, this report implicitly endorsed a 'way of looking' that was to make it harder for teachers to keep their collective professional eye on *learning*.

A focus on achievement (or on its close friend and relation, attainment) necessarily implies concentrating on end-points, on products, on what comes out at the far end when we turn the handle of the schooling machine. In at one end go the 4- or 5-year-olds, who, in the TGAT scheme of things, have yet not reached any recordable levels of attainment, and out, at the other, at the end of Key Stages 1 and 2, come the 7- and 11-year-olds who have reached their attainment targets. The danger of this way of conceptualizing primary education is that it suggests that the processes of teaching and learning are of secondary importance. In focusing on narrow definitions of achievement at particular moments in children's educational careers, we may cultivate a damaging disregard for the quality of everyday life in classrooms and corridors. If primary teachers' mental set towards their pupils is run through with the concept of achievement ('What did you *achieve* at school today?') they may lose sight of a more dynamic, more elusive, but more important aspect of children's lives: their learning. Learning in progress, rather than learning that is all complete, ready to be marked off on the check-list of targets, must be at the centre of the teacher's attention; only then can the teacher engage in the task, that, following Vygotsky[14] and Bruner,[15] we have come to think of as scaffolding, supporting the child's learning in the 'proximal zone of development'.

A recent publication from the School Curriculum and Assessment Authority (SCAA) is an alarming illustration of this very point.[16] This document details a number of 'goals for learning for children by the time they enter compulsory education'. The problem with the document is not the great majority of the goals or outcomes themselves; they are, indeed, desirable. Furthermore, some of them are eminently desirable for the whole of society, not just for the pre-school years (for example, children should be 'sensitive . . . show respect . . . take turns and share fairly'). Other outcomes are not so much desirable as almost inevitable, given the natural course of development (for example, children talking 'about where they live . . . their families and past and present events in their own lives' – what else would they talk about?). But describing the end of the journey (here, the point of entry to compulsory schooling) is not the same as describing the route to be taken on the way. It is self-evident that some desirable outcomes can be achieved by thoroughly undesirable means. For example, the document calls for children to 'recognise letters of the alphabet by shape and sound . . . write their names with appropriate use of upper and lower case letters'. It is not difficult to imagine both appropriate and inappropriate approaches to this end.

The issue is, once again, the relationship between choice and value. Early years educators implementing this document's recommendations have choices to make. Which do they value more: the visible outcome, the capital letter printed on the page; or the transient process, the daily first-hand experiences, through which children learn what writing is for, and how it works? Is it more important to recognize the alphabet by sight and sound, or to understand how writing expresses meaning, and how it reaches an audience? A principled approach to assessment during the pre-school years will not be distracted by the lure of prespecified outcomes in the future, but will attend to the quality of children's experiences in the everyday, in the present tense, where children live and learn.

Another choice: the statutory apparatus of assessment rigorously excludes from its vocabulary any reference to the emotional dimension of teaching and learning. Educators are faced, then, with this choice: they can conduct their own formative and informal assessments in impersonal and detached mode; or they can engage with the elements of feeling inescapably present in every act of learning, of teaching, and of assessing learning. If we choose to ignore this dimension it will not, on that account, disappear; we will simply have closed our eyes to something of enormous importance to our pupils – the emotional impact of our acts of assessment. If we value our pupils as people, and not simply as collections of test scores, levels and targets achieved, we must accept our responsibility, in assessing their learning, for their increased or decreased motivation, their enhanced or eroded self-esteem, their enlarged or diminished desire for understanding.

Observing groups of children in five different schools during the summer term of 1991, the first year of SATs, I noted many incidents that convinced me, once and for all, of the importance of this 'way of looking', a way that includes both cognitive and affective elements of the child's experiences. For example, I watched Susannah, not quite 7 years old, testing her predictions in the notorious science SAT on floating and sinking; I talked to her after the session.

S: I was wrong with the apple.
       I was thinking it would sink. But it floated!
MJD: How did you feel when you were wrong?
S: (*Blushing*) I felt really embarrassed!

In another school, the children were asked to record their personal response to the tasks they had just completed. Andrew wrote:

I was quiut anxious to get a wurd write.

In a third school I watched Chris, aged $7\frac{1}{2}$, spend a frustrating 20 minutes using 1 g and 5 g plastic weights to find the weight of a huge orange he had selected for the floating and sinking experiment. This mission accomplished, with the surreptitious help of his teacher (who was nearly as distressed as he was), he selected for the next test a curl of wood shavings. Placing them in one pan of the beam balance, his face lit up as he saw that the other *did not move*. He rushed to his teacher, who surveyed the scene and sent for the digital scales (who can blame her?). Chris put the shavings on the pan, and examined the display panel. His discovery of weightlessness was confirmed! His teacher tried to set the record straight.

T: What does it weigh?
C: Nothing.
T: It must weigh something. What would *you* say it weighs?
C: Nothing.
T: Can you really have things that weigh nothing?
C: (*Gives in and shakes his head*)
T: Well, you just told me it did! [She is upset, too, in her way.]
T: (*Picks up the results table, where Chris is recording his work, and a pencil*) Come on, let's fill this up quickly. How much did it weigh?
C: Nothing.
T: (*Gives in and writes a zero.*)

During these exchanges Chris's face registered a whole world of emotion: elation, determination, oppression, surrender, distress, and, in his final reaffirmation, a speaking and obstinate conviction. None of this, of course, will have shown up in his recorded levels of attainment. On the other hand, it may well have figured in his teacher's staffroom discussions of SATs, which were, as I observed for myself, equally full of emotion.

During the coffee break that same morning, one teacher, who had been carrying out the English (writing) SAT, addressed the world at large:

'What sort of teacher am I, anyway, if I don't already know which of my children use a dictionary?' This, it seems to me, is a good question to ask about a particular assessment task, but an even better question for helping us to understand the emotions of teachers being required, by statute, to do things to children that are not consistent with their deeply held – if rarely expressed – core values. The value of respect, for children, for teachers – for children's emotional powers, for teachers' expertise and experience – was being denied by the letter of the law, which, rightly or wrongly, the teachers and the children were following. What were the long-term outcomes for Chris, Samantha, Andrew and their teachers, of this approach to assessment? We may speculate: a possible loss of self-esteem? A weakening of the sense of self, which is, as Nias has so convincingly shown,[17] at the centre of teachers' understanding of teaching? A diminution of the desire to explore? A loss of urgency in communicating ideas? A realization that private perceptions have little place in the public world of the classroom? A suppression of spontaneous feelings?

More than fifty years ago, the great sociologist and psychoanalyst Erich Fromm argued that Western culture is characterized by pressures for conformity: 'The suppression of spontaneous feelings, and thereby of the development of genuine individuality, starts very early.'[18] He refers, in a footnote to this sentence, to a research report that shows that the attempts of 3- to 5-year-old children to preserve their spontaneity give rise to the chief conflicts between the children and the authoritative adults. Developing his argument into adult life, Fromm suggests that the discouragement of emotions in general has had some regrettable consequences. Since all creative acts are inseparably linked with emotion, in accepting the standard of thinking and living without emotions, the individual is weakened, 'impoverished and flattened . . . Giving up spontaneity and individuality results in a thwarting of life'.[19]

Fromm's warnings have relevance for my argument here. Assessment practices that do not diminish the spontaneity, or the individuality, or the sense of self of any of the participants are both an expression of value and a principled exercise of choice. This is the crucial distinction between the forms of assessment that are required of teachers, and the forms of assessment that they shape for themselves, in accordance with their innermost beliefs. Assessment practices chosen by teachers who value spontaneous feeling and individual expression will create classrooms where children feel safe to take risks, try out ideas and forge their own understandings. The formal requirements of the statutory programme have the opposite effect. Gipps *et al.* describe a classroom where a child, just about to begin a science task, left his seat to go and fetch a box of magnets. 'When the teacher told him this was not allowed, he was indignant: "But you said that science was about experimenting with things."'[20]

At the beginning of this chapter I quoted from an assessment schedule

(TEDDS) which had made a strong impression on me when I was introduced to it. Less than a week before, I had been observing in a primary
classroom for 4-year-olds (as part of a local authority evaluation programme). There I had spent an amazing quarter of an hour talking to
Lawrence, who was engaged in imaginative play with some small wooden
blocks and a set of miniature figures (play-people). The blocks had been
shaped into some rectangular buildings (a jail) and the play-people represented the prisoner, the guard of the jail, the captain of the jail, the
prisoner's mother, and the prisoner's little children. Lawrence's running
commentary on the drama he was playing out held me spellbound; like
Sloppy (in Dickens's *Our Mutual Friend*) he 'did the police in different
voices' (and all the other characters too). After a particularly violent dis-
agreement between the prisoner and his warder, the prisoner's mother
was denied admittance on her regular visit.

L: . . . and the children can't come in today because they don't
        want to see the blood.
MJD: They'll be upset!
L: No, they'll have nightmares!!
[Soon the mother reasserted her power:]
L: 'She's phoning the prison to say I'm coming back – *now!*'

Some days later, back at my desk, I looked at the categories for spoken language in the TEDDS schedule. (L3), the highest available, is scored when
the child:

Uses regular sentences including correct use of tenses and plurals the
majority of the time e.g. 'The pencil was on the table'.

I looked back, in interest, at my notes on Lawrence. Had he achieved this
level, or had he not? Not consistently, since I had noted his use of the
words 'under-arrested' (and another neat coinage, 'prison-cuffs'). But it
did not seem to matter. I was still convinced that Lawrence's powers to use
language for his own expressive purposes were both strongly developed
and still developing; that the functions for which he used his language
were more important than the form; that Lawrence's intensely dramatic
narrative had nothing to do with grammatical accuracies.

The teachers who designed and implemented TEDDS are, I am absolutely certain, experienced, caring and well intentioned. But this part of
their assessment practice is flawed in a number of significant ways; these
flaws arise not out of malice, or ignorance, but through the fatal discon-
nection of value and choice. I am equally certain that within months of
using TEDDS with children in their own classes, with children whom they
knew as individuals, as meaning makers, as creative artists and experimental scientists, they saw the inadequacies and irrelevance of their

current choices, and returned to the drawing board, so to speak, to revisit the values that have real meaning and relevance to them as teachers.

I have no such certainty about the authors of the National Curriculum assessment requirements. In spite of annual revisions, the forms of statutory assessment now in place still show all the inadequacies that I have described here. They are couched in language that is impersonal and emotionally neutral; they aspire to specificity and accuracy. In this, incidentally, they are doomed to failure; as Schwarzenberger has so succinctly argued, 'the more accurately an attainment can be measured, the less likely is it to reflect genuine understanding'.[21]

Formal assessment practices record the outlines of children's actions, of children's words, not their inner meanings, or their symbolic significance. They focus on what has been achieved in the past, rather than on what is being learned now, or what might be learned tomorrow. They are legitimized by reference to a straight-line model of learning, in which level 2 follows level 1, and gives way in its turn to level 3. Step by step, up the ladder of learning the pupils must go.

And, finally, these practices serve the wrong master. The whole statutory assessment programme has been put in place to satisfy political purposes, not pedagogical ones. Whatever the test results may do for the Secretary of State, or for the Office of Standards in Education, for SCAA, they do, and can do, nothing for children's learning. Desforges argues that the key question to ask of any form of assessment is 'to what degree is this assessment procedure promoting quality learning?'.[22] In the searchlight of this critical question, the statutory assessment requirements are seen for what they are – irrelevant at best, damaging at worst. The good news is that there are alternatives; statutory practices may have been imposed on teachers, but they have not paralysed the profession. Primary teachers' principles may seem to be under threat, but they cannot be struck out by statute. In the assessment practices directed by the National Curriculum orders, we are obliged to use the wrong tools for the wrong job; but in the practice of teacher assessment we can, and will, do better. We are, as we have always been, at liberty to think for ourselves, to reassert our values, and to make principled choices in the interests of children's learning.

Notes

1 Department of Education and Science, *The National Curriculum 5–16: A Consultative Document* (London: HMSO, 1987), p. 11.
2 M.J. Drummond, *Assessing Children's Learning* (London: David Fulton, 1993).
3 G. Blenkin and V. Kelly (eds), *Assessment in Early Childhood Education* (London: Paul Chapman, 1992).
4 C. Gipps, M. Brown, B. McCallum and S. McAlister, *Intuition or Evidence?* (Buckingham: Open University Press, 1995), p. 12.

5 Department of Education and Science, *National Curriculum Task Group on Assessment and Testing: A Report* (London: HMSO, 1988), p. 11.

6 For a fuller discussion of the implications of the reading debate, see M. Styles and M.J. Drummond (eds), *The Politics of Reading* (Cambridge: University of Cambridge Institute of Education and Homerton College, 1993), pp. 8–13.

7 V. Kelly, 'Concepts of assessment: an overview' in G. Blenkin and U. Kelly, *Assessment*, p. 6.

8 M. Armstrong, 'Another way of looking', *Forum*, 33(1), 12 (1990).

9 Department of Education and Science, *English for Ages 5–11* (London: HMSO, 1988), p. 11.

10 Armstrong, 'Another way of looking', p. 10.

11 Ibid., p. 15.

12 Gipps *et al.*, *Intuition or Evidence?*, p. 53.

13 House of Commons Education, Science and Arts Committee, *Achievement in Primary Schools* (London: HMSO, 1986).

14 L. Vygotsky, *Mind in Society* (Cambridge, Mass.: Harvard University Press, 1978).

15 J. Bruner, *Child's Talk: Learning to Use Language* (Oxford: Oxford University Press, 1983).

16 Department for Education and Employment, *Nursery Education: Desirable Outcomes for Children's Learning* (London: DfEE, in conjunction with SCAA, 1996).

17 J. Nias, *Primary Teachers Talking: A Study of Teaching as Work* (London: Routledge, 1989).

18 E. Fromm, *The Fear of Freedom* (London: Routledge & Kegan Paul, 1942), p. 208.

19 Ibid., p. 220.

20 Gipps *et al.*, *Intuition or Evidence?*, p. 65.

21 R. Schwarzenberger, *Targets for Mathematics in Primary Education*, Warwick Seminar on Public Education Policy, Occasional Paper 2 (Stoke on Trent: Trentham Books, 1987), p. 6.

22 C. Desforges, 'Assessment and learning', *Forum*, 34(3), 69 (1992).

6

International comparisons and the quality of primary teaching

Robin Alexander

Introduction

From time to time political imperatives, news values and academic serendipity combine to thrust primary education into the limelight. The year 1996 was in this sense much like 1991: a general election in the offing; a convenient report on primary education; shock headlines; a BBC *Panorama* programme to provide media gravitas; a government initiative to stop the rot; and an anxious academic, worried lest his work be misrepresented.

In 1991 it was the Leeds report;[1] the ensuing government initiative was the so-called 'three wise men' primary discussion paper;[2] and the anxious academic was myself. In 1996 it was the report of the Office for Standards in Education (Ofsted) on international standards in primary education;[3] the rot-stopping government initiative was a national curriculum for the training of teachers; and the anxious academic was David Reynolds. Otherwise the scenario was very much the same. Even the headlines had apparently been recycled: 'Government attacks trendy teachers' . . . 'Happiness but little learning' . . . 'Back to basics' . . . 'Back to tried and tested methods' . . . 'Back to the blackboard at primaries' . . . 'Teachers get a caning from Ken' . . . For Ken, however, read Chris.[4]

There were differences, of course. In 1996 there were three studies, not one: alongside the Ofsted report we had the findings from Taiwan of the International School Effectiveness Research Project (ISERP),[5] together with the Gatsby-funded action research project on primary mathematics teaching in Switzerland, Germany and Britain, led by Sig Prais at the

National Institute for Economic and Social Research in partnership with inspectors and schools in Barking and Dagenham LEA.

More critically, whereas in 1991–2 the Labour opposition had little to say on primary education, by 1996 it was very much in on the act. Indeed, an intriguing consensus had emerged, as political right and left jockeyed for control of territory hitherto held uncontested by the right – 'progressive' teaching methods, incompetent teachers, back to basics, irrelevant and ideologically suspect teacher training. Speaking almost as one, the Secretary of State, the Shadow Secretary of State and the Chief Inspector instructed primary teachers to modify or even abandon their existing practices and adopt the whole-class teaching strategies used in Taiwan, Switzerland, Germany and the Netherlands. The Chief Inspector even put a figure on it: 60 per cent of time for mathematics teaching and 50 per cent for the rest of the curriculum.[6] With the media in attendance, each made the obligatory pilgrimage from Westminster to Barking and Dagenham to applaud the Gatsby teachers' use of a continental version of whole-class teaching. Gillian Shephard and David Blunkett accused teacher trainers of neglecting both the basics and whole-class teaching, and Gillian Shephard announced a national teacher training curriculum which was impressive not so much for its radicalism as for its dishonesty, since there had been a national teacher training curriculum in England and Wales since 1984, defined with increasing precision in DES, DFE and DFEE Circulars 3/84, 24/89, 9/92 and 14/93, and policed first by the Council for the Accreditation of Teacher Education (CATE) and then, from 1994, when CATE started giving advice which the government did not want to hear, by the much more powerful Teacher Training Agency (TTA).

However, the big difference between 1991–2 and 1996 was that by 1996 the debate about primary education had become a global rather than a merely national one. Britain's position in the international league tables of economic performance and competitiveness continued to slide downwards, especially in relation to certain European countries and those of the Pacific Rim. So, too, did children's educational performance, at least as judged by the tests in mathematics and science which had been conducted for the International Association for the Evaluation of Educational Achievement (IEA) and the International Assessment of Educational Progress (IAEP); and this performance gap had apparently increased over the thirty years since the beginning of IEA and IAEP testing. Adding to the gloom, the government's Skills Audit compared the skill levels of Britain's new employees very unfavourably with those of Japan, Singapore, Germany, France and the USA.

At the same time, we were being told that there was a conclusive causal relationship between these measures of national decline and the teaching methods used in the UK's primary schools. Hence Taiwan, Zürich,

Barking and Dagenham, whole-class teaching and Chief Inspector Wood-head's 60 per cent.

There is obviously much to be learned from studying how other countries educate their younger children, and policy-makers' recognition of this is to be welcomed, for public debate about primary education in the UK has been as parochial as it has been polarized and repetitive. However, in this chapter I wish to sound a note of caution, particularly in relation to what we might call the 'new' comparative paradigm of inputs, indicators, outcomes and effectiveness measures. I shall also consider the current political enthusiasm for whole-class teaching, and in this context will refer briefly to the Barking and Dagenham primary schools involved in the Gatsby project.

International comparisons, old and new

It has become almost obligatory for comparativists to quote turn-of-the-century educational administrator and comparativist Michael Sadler:[7]

> The practical value of studying in a right spirit and with scholarly accuracy the working of foreign systems of education is that it will result in our being better fitted to study and understand our own.

So far, so good (though we might ponder for a moment on what Sadler meant by 'a right spirit'), but that sentence was preceded by one which was slightly more contentious:

> In studying foreign systems of education we should not forget that the things outside the schools matter even more than the things inside the schools, and govern and interpret the things inside.

This almost anthropological conviction in the cultural location of human activity in turn informed his celebrated antipathy to the kind of cultural borrowing which we are being encouraged to indulge in today with respect to Taiwan and Switzerland:

> No other nation, by imitating a little bit of German organisation, can thus hope to achieve a true reproduction of the spirit of German institutions. The fabric of an organisation practically forms one whole. That is its merits, and its danger. It must either be taken in all, or left unimitated.

And:

> All good and true education is an expression of national life and character.

These lines were written nearly a century ago, in the context of anxiety about how Britain's education system should counter Germany's growing industrial and commercial supremacy. We have been there before, then: yesterday Prussia and Germany, today the Pacific Rim, Switzerland, and Germany again.

With our late twentieth-century multi-cultural consciousness we might balk at Sadler's assumption of national cultural homogeneity. And swept along on the tide of globalization as we also are, we might find his purist rejection of cultural borrowing rather quaint. Nevertheless, there are important challenges to any comparativist, in any time or place, in what Sadler asserts. Is the primary purpose of comparative study to understand other education systems or to extrapolate from them? Do we analyse education elsewhere in order better to understand our own practices, or in order to change them?

Here, if you like, is the main fault-line in the current literature. On the one hand there is the long-established academic community of comparativists, with their own societies, journals and conferences. They may have their disagreements and debates about purposes and methods, but they are united in their conviction that comparative study is pursued primarily for its own sake, that pursuit of understanding comes first and policy applications second. When you read the studies by Patricia Broadfoot and her colleagues, going back to the 1970s, of primary teachers and teaching in England and France,[8] or the analysis of preschool education in Japan, China and the United States by Tobin *et al.*,[9] or James Muckle's account of his term spent teaching and observing in Moscow's School No. 1937 in the early days of *perestroika*,[10] you cannot but reflect at the same time on how schooling is conducted in Britain. Comparative studies like these enrich your understanding of education here at the same time as they enlarge your apprehension of what happens elsewhere in the world. However, it is but a short step from a comparative mode which is *descriptive* to one which is *evaluative*, and to judgements about those things which another country does not just differently but better or worse than our own. And it is a short step again to prescriptions for change. Yet prescription, if it is offered in mainstream comparative education, tends to be tentative rather than definitive, and is a spin-off rather than the primary purpose of the research.

In sharp contrast there is the new and fast-growing community of international school effectiveness researchers, dedicated to finding what patterns of teaching and school organization work best and encouraging schools, and even governments, to adopt them. They are an offshoot of the school effectiveness/school improvement movement of the 1980s, which at that stage was less an international community than a number of groups working in parallel in different countries.[11] Now networked, they argue that there is no point in the international comparative study of education unless you are prepared to act on what you find out. Their endeavour is quantitative and quasi-scientific. They seek out policy-makers and are sought out by them.

The fault-line which I have identified seems to be recognized by those on either side of it. Altbach and Kelly identify several traditions, or theoretical/methodological standpoints, which have shaped the discipline of comparative education: idiosyncratic 'travellers' tales', the more normative and policy-directed 'educational lending and borrowing' which Michael Sadler was one of the first to resist, historical and cultural analysis, the social sciences, economics (with a strong dose of human capital theory, especially in studies of developing countries) and psychometrics.[12]

However, though this might be regarded as a continuum, an invitation to interdisciplinarity and eclecticism, others see it more in terms of opposing paradigms. Thus, writing before the current vogue for school effectiveness research but in the context of the IEA and OECD studies which have fed it, the comparativist Edmund King saw this emergent tradition as positivist, determinist and manipulative.[13] For their part, Reynolds and Farrell, in the Ofsted review of educational achievement and effectiveness in Britain and other countries, in effect blame comparativists like King for the fact that there are so few convincing explanations for the poor showing of English pupils in international comparisons of achievement. Reynolds and Farrell write despairingly of:

> the frankly inept contribution which the comparative education discipline has made over time . . . the presence of a large body of theories, without any apparent empirical backing . . . a large range of descriptive case studies of individual schools which it is impossible to synchronise together because there are no common measures of outcomes or processes utilised . . . descriptions of the range of educational, political, economic and cultural phenomena within different countries, with no attempt ever made to assess the contribution of the educational system as against that of other factors.[14]

I am afraid that I part company with Reynolds and Farrell at this point, though I understand their frustration that we seem to have come so far and learned so little. Consider what they seem to be saying: that there is no place for speculative theory in our attempts to understand other cultures and how education is conceived of and undertaken within them; that unless individual researchers in different traditions and different countries coordinate their activities within a common analytical framework they might as well give up; that educational phenomena can validly be compared only in terms of measurable processes and outcomes; that political, cultural, economic and educational aspects of a society are not worth studying unless they can be factor-analysed.

This, it seems to me, is the subtext of the policy-makers' enthusiasm for school effectiveness research. It is not just that they can bypass the methodological caveats which researchers in this tradition properly and inevitably voice and translate the studies' factors, indicators and statistics into declarations like Chris Woodhead's 60 per cent. The view I have quoted may also unwittingly legitimate the current official tendency in the UK to dismiss as 'irrelevant' all educational research which is not consistent with the prevailing political viewpoint.

Yet, though by criticizing the 'old' comparative education Reynolds and Farrell seem to be saying that they are not comparativists, that is surely what they are. Predominantly quantitative studies like ISERP are no less immune to the kinds of problems which mainstream comparativists such as Harold Noah[15] warn against than those which use the 'soft' methods of ethnography: problems such as using the educational practices of another country to make a political case for change in one's own, when one's account of those practices may be methodologically flawed; misinterpretation or over-interpretation of results in a research field whose inherent weaknesses are compounded by barriers of culture and language; ethnocentrism – viewing another culture through the lens of one's own – something none of us can escape from; and, of course, cultural borrowing.

A classic example which combines several of these problems – and also provides an intriguing double irony in the present context – is the American 'open education' movement of the 1960s and 1970s which Diane Ravitch charted over a decade ago.[16] Indeed, there will be many who, like myself, witnessed the extraordinary enthusiasm of a generation of American teachers and academics for precisely that brand of English primary education – what we called progressivism and what the Americans called 'open education' – that the Black Paper authors and their successors most strongly deplored. It was exported, lock, stock and barrel, from Oxfordshire, Leicestershire and the West Riding to Connecticut, Illinois, North Dakota, New Jersey and Massachussetts, and it did not work.

The double irony, in case it is not readily apparent, is, first, the way educators in the world's most successful economy showed such unbridled enthusiasm for a system of primary education which even then was being accused by the Black Paper authors of being responsible for Britain's economic – and indeed moral – decline; and second, that we seem to be witnessing yet again these same processes of over-interpretation and naive cultural borrowing, though this time in reverse, as politicians and Ofsted inspectors fall over each other in the rush to go to Barking and Dagenham and endorse as preferred practice for England and Wales' 20,000 primary schools an unfinished experiment in mathematics teaching taking place in just six of those schools. Do the new cultural borrowers really believe that there are no examples of highly successful whole-class teaching to be found anywhere else in England? Or is it just that they are determined to ignore all research evidence that does not put English primary education in a bad light?

But the ironies and complexities of cultural borrowing reach deeper still. Brian Holmes shows how the establishment of national systems of elementary education in Europe and North America was in part influenced by travellers' tales from England, France, Switzerland, Italy, Holland and Prussia,[17] and to this day, despite the differences, there are notable similarities at elementary level world-wide, especially in respect of the curriculum, where the dominance of the three Rs is more or less a universal phenomenon.[18] At the same time, the French, English and other colonial powers were busy imposing their versions of elementary education on their imperial outposts. And as an example of how intertwined cultural borrowing and cultural imperialism in education can become, Tobin *et al.* point out that the large classes and whole-class teaching in Japanese elementary schools which Western educators, including Ofsted,[19] so admire, are not indigenous to that country, but were imported from the USA and consolidated during the period of post-war occupation in the 1940s. The traditional Japanese education, they say, 'emphasized small classes, individual tutorials, hands-on training and learning through apprenticeship'.[20]

Thus it may be that what some today so admire as a model for English primary schools is a version of something that started in England and has returned a century later via the USA and Japan, polished and perfected.

However, before the advocates of whole-class teaching in large classes claim that their point is proved, they should consider the example of India, where the legacy of British elementary education under the Raj fails to deliver literacy to all primary children, in part (though only in part) because of over-large classes and insufficient resources. They might also note my experience of meeting teachers and officials in France – long seen as the archetype of centralized planning and 'formal' pedagogy – who were keen to talk about activity methods, discovery learning and the developmental curriculum. Indeed, if you read the text of France's 1989 Education Framework Act, the *loi Jospin*, and consider the three cycles into which French primary education is now divided, you will be struck by the strength of the new emphasis on developmental considerations: 'L'organisation en cycles offre les souplesses indispensables pour respecter la diversité des élèves, leurs demands, leurs attentes, leur rythme de développement'.[21] So, notwithstanding our ailing economy, our declining levels of educational attainment, and our masochistic conviction that our schools are far worse than those of our competitors, others apparently believe that the ideas which shaped post-war British primary education may have something to commend them.

The quest for effectiveness

I have noted that the most recent addition to comparative educational study is school effectiveness research, and that the apparent certainty and clarity with which it identifies and then measures its factors, causes and effects makes it politically much more attractive than mainstream classroom research, both quantitative and – especially – qualitative. However, its account of classroom processes needs to guard very carefully against the kind of statistical reductionism which can be observed, for example, in some of the OECD studies on 'indicators' of educational quality, which measure only the measurable, and in doing so focus almost exclusively on inputs and outputs.[22]

David Reynolds and the ISERP team have made two well-publicized contributions to the current debate. One is the review for Ofsted of international surveys of educational achievement.[23] The other is their comparative study of school effectiveness in nine countries, one of which is Britain.[24]

The Ofsted review lists and summarizes the outcomes of the IEA and IAEP test programmes which started thirty years ago and concludes that these justify serious concern about the performance of English children in science and mathematics, especially the latter, and above all in arithmetic. The authors then speculate on the possible reasons for Britain's relatively poor performance and consistent decline.

I want to make two brief but fundamental observations about the Ofsted survey, with both of which I know that its authors agree. First, the IEA and IAEP test programmes are deeply flawed technically. Reynolds and Farrell themselves carefully catalogue problems of poor sampling, missing data, excessively variable response rates, and lack of between-country comparability in test items and administration procedures which are so serious as to make one wonder whether the test results were worth reporting at all. Wendy Keys claims that the Third International Mathematics and Science Survey (TIMMS) of 500,000 children at ages 12–14 will avoid all these problems,[25] and on that basis will feature in the December 1996 edition of OECD's *Education at a Glance*.[26]

My other comment about the Ofsted survey is this. When, in the last part of their study, Reynolds and Farrell consider explanations for Britain's apparently poor showing in this somewhat suspect testing programme, they are able to offer not empirically demonstrated proof of a cause–effect relationship between the factors they identify and the IEA/IAEP test scores, but a series of hypotheses which have yet to be tested and on only some of which there is published evidence of some kind. Though the authors do in fact make very clear the speculative nature of their analysis, this is not, by and large, how it has been treated in public discussion ('Standards plummet' . . . 'Report blames trendy teachers' . . . 'Minister promises training shake-up').

Rather more cautiously than this, the report recommends that we should be prepared to experiment with alternative ways of teaching, though not to the extent of exchanging one uncritically adopted fad for another. More important, however, is their argument that we should fundamentally rethink how we define children's abilities and needs and the extent to which we differentiate between these in our teaching. This is very much in line with a consistent strand in the evidence from school inspections and classroom research which has pointed to a pervasive problem of low expectations and an obsession with children's 'problems' rather than their potential.[27]

As for the ISERP proper, this requires a much fuller examination than is possible in this context, so again I will limit myself to two basic observations, this time one technical and the other conceptual.

My technical reservation is that because this study seeks to be generalizable and representative, rather than indicative, we shall need to look closely at the sampling and measurement methods adopted. The first ISERP study focused on the performance of high- and low-attaining 7-year-olds in mathematics in between five and twelve schools in each of nine countries. The reasons for these choices were methodological rather than educational: to maximize variance on the dependent variables and to minimize 'problems of controlling for home and external factors'. However, it is extremely important to note the political ramifications of this innocent technical comment: by minimizing a factor methodologically, you minimize it substantively and politically.

The sample size meant that claims about the impact of the different effectiveness factors were based on what went on in just 12 out of the 25,000 primary schools in the UK and 12 out of the 80,000 elementary schools in the USA, a country where sampling problems are exacerbated by colossal cultural diversity and an exceptional degree of decentralization not just from federal to state levels, but also from state to school board. Moreover, since the UK sample included Northern Ireland and Scotland as well as England and Wales, the scope in this study for accessing empirically the peculiarly English brand of 'progressive' primary practice which has now been fingered as the principal culprit in the UK's educational failure was, to say the least, extremely limited.

Another technical reservation one might make is that the effectiveness factors were identified on the basis of questionnaire responses. The researchers were asked to rank-order a list of dimensions in terms of their capacity to differentiate between successful and less successful schools. Thus, notwithstanding their common-sense validity, we should note that the factors which emerged from this process were those that researchers believed were the most significant, not those which had been shown empirically to be most significant:[28]

- a strong commitment to academic goals;
- a cohesive, consistent and stable school environment;
- schooling which is proactive rather than reactive;
- effective management of time;
- good teacher–teacher relationships;
- highly interactive classroom teaching.

The conceptual point to be made about the ISERP study concerns its handling of the notion of culture. David Reynolds, Bert Creemers and their colleagues have stressed the probable influence on pupil attainment in a country such as Taiwan of matters like teachers' high status, the narrow range of goals and tasks with which primary schools deal, the cultural stress on self-improvement and respect for education, and the belief that all children, given hard work and good teaching, can succeed.

These kinds of messages from comparative study are extremely important, and they contrast very markedly, as many have recently noted, with attitudes and practices in some schools in England and in some parts of English society. We can and must learn from this. However, at the same time the ISERP research appears to conceive of culture as being somehow outside or apart from education:

> We do not . . . know yet what is the exact contribution of the *educational* system and of the *cultural* and *social* systems to the very high levels of educational success enjoyed by other societies, although most observers would credit the system at least as much as the society.[29]

To separate the cultural, educational and social into three apparently independent and free-wheeling 'systems', which can then be translated into a collection of factors for the purposes of statistical correlation, seems to me to be conceptually untenable. Life in schools and classrooms is an aspect of our wider society, not separate from it: a culture does not stop at the school gates. The character and dynamics of school life are shaped by the values which shape other aspects of our national life. The strengths of our primary schools are the strengths of our society; their weaknesses are our society's weaknesses; their tensions mirror the fractured and unstable nature of British culture in the late twentieth century.

To illustrate the importance of this issue, we might note that the striking feature of the ISERP Taiwanese study was the way the values of classroom, home, government and society coincided. In England, our education system, like our society, is shot through with conflicts of a fundamental kind, and politicians' claim that there is a 'new consensus' about primary education is really no more than an acknowledgement that it is politically expedient in the short term for government and opposition to sing the same tune.

This claim of consensus, incidentally, is particularly rich coming from a government which has used confrontation to whip teachers and teacher trainers into line, and which has created an inspection system which is far more prescriptive and punitive than those operated by most of our economic competitors. As Brian Simon points out,[30] one of the sharpest conflicts of all is in educational policy itself: between the market culture of freedom and competitiveness, and an unprecedented degree of top-down regulation and control.

The compartmentalization of culture is unsatisfactory not only in a broad conceptual sense. If the argument were only one of how the word 'culture' should be defined it would be hardly worth making, in this context anyway. More important are the educational consequences of this view. At national level it enables governments to legitimate their claim that questions of quality in education can be resolved by attacking pedagogy while ignoring structure and resources. It allows them to deny that a government's broader social and economic policies impact in any way on what teachers do, or can do, in the classroom. At classroom level it encourages the view that pedagogy carries no educational messages or values of itself, but is merely a value-neutral vehicle for transmitting curricular content; and it discourages vital questions about the importance of 'fit' between pedagogy, the children being taught, and the knowledge domains from which curriculum experiences are drawn. Effective teaching arises from attention to cultural, psychological, epistemological and situational considerations, not merely organizational and technical ones.[31]

Thus, in this context of the interest in primary education in countries as culturally remote from our own as Taiwan and Japan, treating culture as an independent variable in a statistical calculation encourages the assumption that you can detach an educational strategy from the values and conditions which give it meaning and ensure its success, transpose it to a context where these may be diametrically opposed, and yet expect it to deliver the same results.

Whole-class teaching: the current totem of effectiveness

All of which brings me to whole-class teaching, which, alongside a good dose of the basics, is the current panacea not just for effective primary education but also, apparently, for a highly trained workforce and an economy as lean, competitive and successful as any on the Pacific Rim.

In my own current research I have gathered a wealth of observational data, including many hours of videotape, from primary classrooms in countries as different as England, Russia, India, France and the United States. I have observed whole-class teaching taking place, in some form, in most of the classrooms I have visited. The first point to be made is this:

'whole-class teaching' sounds precise enough as a type of teaching method, and tough enough as a stick with which to beat teachers and teacher trainers, but empirical study shows that it covers a very wide variety of practices, takes many different forms and serves many different purposes. This prompts me to ask which of the many available versions of whole-class teaching Chief Inspector Woodhead wishes to see being used for 60 per cent of mathematics teaching and 50 per cent of the rest of the time; or which of them should feature in the national curriculum for teacher training.

The second point arises if we approach the problem from a different angle – that of the economic success which whole-class teaching is supposed to deliver. Countries like Germany, Switzerland and Japan have several things in common: they are among the richest and most highly competitive of the world's high-income industrial market economies; they have some of the world's highest graduation rates from secondary and higher education; and, as it happens, they all use a great deal of whole-class teaching in their primary schools. But consider also India, Bangladesh, Zaire, Malawi and Vietnam: they are all economies with low incomes, low GDP and low GNP; they have some of the world's lowest secondary and higher graduation rates; and, once again, they all use a great deal of whole-class teaching in their primary schools.

Thus, because whole-class teaching is one of the two near-universals of primary education on this planet, the other being an emphasis on the three Rs,[32] it can be made to correlate, world-wide, with every level of educational and economic performance – high, low, middling, and all points in between – which we may care to identify.

If this is so, then three conclusions follow. First, whole-class teaching, as such, cannot be defined as the magic ingredient x of high educational performance, let alone of economic prosperity. Quite apart from what I have just said, consider the USA, where there is a great deal of group and individual work in elementary schools but which is well ahead economically, and Russia, which uses whole-class teaching extremely effectively to achieve high standards at an early age in the basics, yet whose economy is in deep trouble. Second, therefore, and surely obvious to all but those whose level of responsibility for our education system exceeds their understanding of it, educational success, like educational failure, is multifactorial, and (Michael Sadler again) the things outside the school matter as much as those inside the school. Third, if we want to understand how whole-class teaching contributes both to relative success and relative failure in educational performance, then we need to move beyond the talismanic label and examine its constituents.

I suggest that whole-class teaching comprises three simultaneous levels or dimensions of activity. First, the teacher uses a particular organizational device, that of working on a single task with all the pupils at the same time.

This is the minimal definition of whole-class teaching, and the one on which the political advocates of this method tend to fix. Even then, they manage to be more minimal still, insisting that the only way to teach the whole class is from the front of the room. The teachers in my own international data, fortunately, were not bound by the teacher training national curriculum and felt free to stand at the back, the front or the middle, or even to move around.

Second, central in every case is discourse between teacher and pupils. The teacher deploys a variety of ways of asking questions, handling answers, explaining, instructing, giving feedback, and getting pupils to volunteer and explore their ideas. Such discourse can vary enormously in style, substance, pace and, of course, quality.

The discourse also varies in *intention*: on the basic continuum offered by Her Majesty's Inspectorate (HMI) in the 1978 primary survey,[33] it can be *didactic* or *exploratory*. 'Didactic discourse' on the HMI continuum can be sharpened up into *direct instruction* as defined a year later by Rosenshine.[34] He restricted his definition to:

> didactic ends, that is instruction towards rational, specific, analytic goals . . . instruction is defined as structured but not authoritarian, questions are pitched so as to enable pupils to produce a high proportion of correct answers, and feedback . . . is immediate and academically oriented.

Or, as another way of looking at pedagogic intention in teacher–pupil discourse you might consider the two clusters which emerged from our ESRC-funded CICADA analysis of the discourse in 60 lessons given by 30 English primary teachers in 1986, 1988 and 1992. One group of teachers tended towards discourse which was dominated by directions, commands and judgements, and which involved setting up a learning task, standing back while children undertook it, intervening only where necessary, and providing feedback. The other group tended towards discourse which emphasized explaining, exploring, asking questions and eliciting ideas and information. In the first (cluster 1), the discourse was essentially a device for managing the learning task; in the second (cluster 2) it was intrinsic to it. Neither was associated exclusively with the supposed polarities of whole-class teaching or individual attention, though the cluster 2 teachers had a greater proportion of whole-class interactions than did cluster 1. The clusters, incidentally, were stable over time, despite the apparently disruptive impact of the National Curriculum.[35]

Whichever mode we adopt for analysing teacher–pupil discourse in a whole-class setting, we need to note that whole-class teaching need not exclude other kinds of activity – collaborative group work, for example. Such activity is an adjunct of the whole-class teaching, not something apart from it, still less – as is sometimes argued – philosophically opposed to it.

The third dimension of whole-class teaching is the one least attended to in both public discussion and educational research. Whatever the purpose and manner of his or her interaction, the teacher conveys not only ideas, information and instructions but also values and expectations. These range from requirements of an instrumental and explicit kind relating to pupils' behaviour, and to their progress and attainment in the subjects taught, to the somewhat more subliminal values concerning the nature and worthwhileness of different ways of thinking, knowing and understanding.

Moreover, in this matter the teacher is not necessarily autonomous. The method chosen – whether whole-class teaching or something else – is a necessary response to the particular circumstances in which teacher and children find themselves.

These three pedagogic dimensions – *organization, discourse*, and *values* – underpin all teaching strategies, not merely whole-class teaching. In attempting to evaluate the impact of a teacher's actions, we need to explicate the character of each and assess their congruence. In coining the label 'class enquirer', the ORACLE team presaged this line of analysis in respect of two of the three dimensions (though not the third), arguing the primacy of discourse, and specifically what they called 'higher-order cognitive interaction',[36] an idea which has now been recycled by the ISERP team and the Gatsby project, both of which talk about 'interactive whole-class teaching'.

However, the apparent precision of 'interactive whole-class teaching' also needs to be unpicked. In the classic continental version of direct instruction the learning steps are frequent and shallow, so as to enable all the children to move on together. Thus, overall, the interaction may be 'higher-order' but each of its individual segments may have a relatively low level of demand in order to maximize the chances of success for all children in the class.

If we consider the three dimensions further, we observe that the second and third are not exclusive concomitants of the first, but are in fact aspects of a variety of teaching strategies. We could take the ORACLE labels and interchange them to illustrate this point. The ORACLE 'class enquirer' fits the ISERP/Gatsby idea of 'interactive whole-class teaching', but there are also class instructors and class monitors, just as there are group enquirers and group monitors as well as the ORACLE 'group instructors'.

If, further, you set the three dimensions against what we know about how children learn, you may well conclude that it is the character of the discourse and the nature of the values conveyed and exchanged in teaching which are the more critical ingredients, however important the organizational strategy may be – and this quite apart from such issues as subject matter, task design, assessment and so on, which are equally fundamental to our consideration of teaching quality.

Moreover, this is not just a matter of analytic clarity: there are important moral choices at stake. If the teaching methods of the admired Taiwanese, Japanese or Swiss classrooms are indeed *manifestations* of cultural values rather than merely – as in the ISERP analysis – *responses* to them, then we need to be clear whether, in the proper pursuit of pedagogic efficiency, we wish to import, along with the method, everything else that the method conveys to the pupils who experience it: messages about, for example, the extent to which knowledge is open or bounded, provisional or uncontestable; about how ideas should be handled; about the kinds of authority which teachers and curricula embody and the extent to which they may be questioned; about how individuals and groups should relate to each other; about the balance of individual autonomy and collective responsibility; about what counts as successful learning; and about what it means to be educated. We should also be alert to the power of pedagogy to deliver messages which may or may not be consistent with the educational goals which we espouse, just as we should understand that in importing a teaching method which we find admirable we may also import values with which we may be rather less comfortable. This, I stress, is an appeal not to covert xenophobia but to a proper understanding of the relationship between pedagogy and culture.

It is, then, to the *generic properties* of strategies such as whole-class teaching that we should be attending in this necessary debate about improving primary education, and in our wholly proper desire to draw on international comparisons in order to effect such improvements.

I said that I would return to the Gatsby classrooms of Barking and Dagenham, which in 1996 were being paraded as the new template for effective primary teaching to replace the 1980s model of 'good primary practice' which I examined in the Leeds research.[37] The first comment to make in the light of our analysis is that we have here just one version of the strategy of whole-class teaching of the many which are available. Presumably, nobody involved in that project would be happy if this version were defined as the model for all teachers and all situations. In any case, every Gatsby lesson combined, as a matter of policy, the project's version of whole-class teaching with other methods. The pilgrims, in search of a simpler gospel, ignored this.

The second point to make is one that the Gatsby team will confirm from their experience, as I can from my observations: namely, that it is easy enough to import from central Europe the *organizational* element of whole-class teaching which so impressed Chris Woodhead, David Blunkett and Gillian Shephard, but it is much more difficult to import the *discourse* with which, at best, the continental tradition of whole-class teaching is associated.

At best, then, this discourse is brisk, energetic, searching and articulate, and is informed by the teacher's deep understanding of the subject being taught. And there is an absence – which many teachers in England and Wales would find surprising – of the special teacherly tone and vocabulary which are such distinctive features of many English primary schools and American elementary schools, especially where early years teaching is concerned: slow, careful, oblique ('somebody's using a big voice' instead of 'Gillian, you're shouting: stop it'), collective ('we' rather than the more confrontational 'you'), encouraging, patient, euphemistic, self-conscious and, above all, different from the language of the world outside school. What you often hear instead in continental classrooms is a direct, businesslike quality in the exchanges between teachers and pupils which on the teacher's side some here would find brusque, even brutal, but which is countered by pupils' readiness to stand up and give a confident account of what they know and how they think.

This matter of congruence or incongruence between the language of the classroom and the language of life outside school is significant. Consider the French classrooms which feature in the studies of Broadfoot and her colleagues,[38] or the French and Italian classrooms observed by HMI.[39] What is going on there between teachers and children is embedded in a culture in which words, reasoning and argument are historically of profound importance, in which the sound and quality of the native language, and the individual's ability to use it, matter a great deal, and in which daily life, whether in the classroom, the family, the restaurant or the street, is in part a celebration of the power and excitement of talk. Can we say that of England, with its poles of braying, mumbling diffidence, estuarial incoherence and yobbishness? Or indeed of many English classrooms?

In this context it is pertinent to report that when I analyse my own international data in terms of the ten generic curriculum activities which emerged from the Leeds research – reading, writing, talk, collaboration, construction and so on – I find that on a simple quantitative measure the ratio of structured talk to writing is very different in the French and Russian classrooms to those in England: much more writing in the English classrooms, much more structured talk in the French and Russian ones. Is this significant? I think it is, culturally no less than educationally.

You can import the organizational form of continental whole-class teaching readily enough, but the discourse, and the values in which the discourse is embedded, are quite another matter.

Conclusion

The UK is confronted by some very serious problems, which, notwithstanding the shakiness of some of the evidence, compel our attention. It is underachieving economically; many of the pupils in its schools – that notorious long 'tail' which figures in all the international performance studies – are underachieving educationally; there is insufficient fit between the skills and knowledge the economy needs and the skills and knowledge with which pupils are leaving school; and the primary stage of education appears to be less effective than it should in providing the foundations of literacy and numeracy upon which later education depends. All this is now well-worked territory. We can disagree about the extent and details of each of these problems, while agreeing that they are real and serious.

The question of causes and solutions, however, is much more difficult. What we witnessed in 1996–7 was not the careful and honest analysis which this matter requires, but government and opposition competing for quick electoral advantage in the run-up to the general election. History, as I said at the beginning, repeats itself – as in 1991–2, so in 1996–7. To identify primary teaching methods as an element in the problem is reasonable: teaching, fortunately, does make a difference. To identify a single model of teaching as the solution is premature and naive. It is not just that the discussions about whole-class teaching in documents such as the Reynolds and Farrell Ofsted report are – as its authors are at pains to stress – speculative. It is also the case that the ubiquity of whole-class teaching means that, internationally, it correlates as closely with low achievement as with high. And I say that as someone who, like Chris Woodhead, has gone on record as arguing that whole-class teaching could be more fully exploited in primary schools than it sometimes is. It *is* a vital part of the primary teacher's repertoire, but so too is effectively conducted group work, both teacher-led and collaborative.

Moreover, as Jim Rose, Chris Woodhead and I wrote in the 1992 primary discussion paper:[40]

> It is fashionable to blame the Plowden Report for what are perceived as the current ills of primary education . . . If things have gone wrong – and the word 'if' is important – then scapegoating is not the answer. All those responsible for administering and delivering our system of primary education need to look carefully at the part they may have played.

By which we meant this: teaching methods, the curriculum, the way schools are managed, the way LEAs are run, the way teachers are trained and supported, the levels of funding, the distribution and use of resources, the mechanisms for inspection and quality assurance, the policies, demands and requirements of central government, all have an impact on the quality and outcomes of children's learning. And if one part of the system is weak, then it weakens the others.

If, however, we acknowledge that pedagogy, as just one of these elements, is nevertheless an extremely important one (which it is), and if we want pedagogy to be used to the best effect, we need to examine it not in terms of the current shibboleth of whole-class teaching, but in a way which gets at all its dimensions and forms and examines the full range of possibilities open to us. By taking whole-class teaching as an example, I have tried to show that to understand a teaching method, let alone to exploit its full potential, you need to penetrate below the surface level of organization, important though that is, to the deeper levels of discourse and values. In particular, I have emphasized, as I and other educational researchers have been doing for many years, the central role in learning of high-quality classroom discourse. This should be a feature of whole-class teaching, but the two are not synonymous; high-quality discourse should be a feature of other methods as well, and if we can shift our attention from the organizational form to such generic properties of effective teaching, we may be on to something much more promising as a route to improved standards.

This is where comparative research comes in. For although international comparisons can help us to enlarge our vocabulary of pedagogical possibilities, pedagogy is a particularly weak element in both the old and the new comparative research. In the old, it is frequently ignored altogether. In the new, it tends to be reduced to what can be measured – time on task, for example (and even that has its problems). And in both, the subtlety and many-layered character of classroom processes is lost and a teaching method is reduced from many dimensions to one.

When that happens, the problems of cultural borrowing are compounded. I have suggested that the comparativists' unease about cultural borrowing needs to be tempered by the recognition that this, historically, is in part how education systems – and societies – have developed. We can, must and do learn from others. Nevertheless, history also teaches us that simple 'off-the-peg' borrowing of educational practices, of the kind that is currently being commended for primary schools, may not work, because it treats such practices as value-neutral and fails to explore the way they relate to the wider culture of which classroom life is a part. History suggests, too, that primary teaching in England has been excessively influenced by borrowing and lending of another kind – the arbitrary swings of the pendulum of educational fashion.

There is another, and final, angle on all this. My theme has been a response to a current political preoccupation – the relationship between primary teaching methods, educational standards and the economy. In these vital matters I have tried to be constructive as well as critical. But defining problems is not a government or opposition monopoly. There are many other problems in our society besides our position in international league tables of economic and educational performance, pressing though these particular problems undoubtedly are: the condition of families, communities and cities; of workplaces and our environment; the way people relate to each other; the way, collectively, Britain relates to other countries, especially those on the other side of the Channel and those at the lower end of that economic league table; our political system, and the moral standpoint which, for better or worse, it exemplifies. How does primary education stand in relation to these problems? Is it to be blamed for them, too? Or might government and opposition acknowledge, for a change, that in encouraging children to think independently and critically, and in attending to their inner lives, to their social and personal development and to their welfare, as well as to their manifest need to be literate and numerate, British primary schools may actually have done the state some service?

Acknowledgement

This paper is a considerably shortened version of my *Other Primary Schools and Ours: Hazards of International Comparison* (Warwick: Centre for Research in Elementary and Primary Education, 1996).

Notes

1 R.J. Alexander, *Primary Education in Leeds* (Leeds: University of Leeds, 1991).
2 R.J. Alexander, J. Rose and C. Woodhead, *Curriculum Organisation and Classroom Practice in Primary Schools* (London: HMSO, 1992).
3 D. Reynolds and S. Farrell, *Worlds Apart? A Review of International Surveys of Educational Achievement Involving England* (London: Ofsted, 1996).
4 Kenneth Clarke, Secretary of State for Education and Science in 1991; Chris Woodhead, HM Chief Inspector of Schools in 1996.
5 D. Reynolds and C. Teddlie, *World Class Schools: A Preliminary Analysis from the International School Effectiveness Research Project (ISERP)* (Newcastle upon Tyne: University of Newcastle upon Tyne Department of Education, 1995); D. Creemers, D. Reynolds, S. Stringfield and C. Teddlie, 'World class schools: some further findings', paper presented to the annual conference of the American Educational Research Association, New York.
6 C. Woodhead, Interview on 'Hard Lessons', *Panorama*, BBC TV (3 June 1996).
7 M. Sadler, 'The unrest in secondary education in Germany and elsewhere' in Board of Education, *Education in Germany: Special Reports on Education Subjects, Vol. 9* (London: HMSO, 1902).
8 P. Broadfoot, *Education, Assessment and Society* (Buckingham: Open University Press, 1996); P. Broadfoot and M. Osborn, with M. Gilly and A. Bûcher, *Perceptions of Teaching: Primary School Teachers in England and France* (London: Cassell, 1993).
9 J.J. Tobin, D.Y. Wu and D.H. Davidson, *Preschool in Three Cultures: Japan, China and the United States* (New Haven: Yale University Press, 1989).
10 J. Muckle, *Portrait of a Soviet School under Glasnost* (London: Macmillan, 1990).
11 P. Sammons, J. Hillman and P. Mortimore, *Key Characteristics of Effective Schools: A Review of School Effectiveness Research* (London: Ofsted, 1995); D. Reynolds,

B.P.M. Creemers, P.S. Nesselrodt, E.C. Shaffer, S. Stringfield and C. Teddlie, *Advances in School Effectiveness Research and Practice* (Oxford: Pergamon, 1994).

12 P.G. Altbach and G.P. Kelly (eds), *New Approaches to Comparative Education* (Chicago: University of Chicago Press, 1986).

13 E.J. King, *Other Schools and Ours: Comparative Studies for Today* (London: Holt, Rinehart and Winston, 1979).

14 Reynolds and Farrell, *Worlds Apart?*, p. 54.

15 H.J. Noah, 'The use and abuse of comparative education' in Altbach and Kelly, *New Approaches to Comparative Education*.

16 D. Ravitch, *The Troubled Crusade: American Education, 1945–1980* (New York: Basic Books, 1983).

17 B. Holmes, *Comparative Education: Some Considerations of Method* (London: Allen & Unwin, 1981).

18 A. Benavot, Y.-K. Cha, D. Kames, J.W. Meyer and S.-Y. Wong, 'Knowledge for the masses: world models and national curricula, 1920–1986', *American Sociological Review*, 56 (1991), pp. 85–100.

19 Department for Education, *Teaching and Learning in Japanese Elementary Schools* (London: DFE, 1992).

20 Tobin *et al.*, *Preschool in Three Cultures*, p. 220.

21 Ministère de l'Éducation Nationale, *Programmes de l'École Primaire* (Paris: Ministère de l'Éducation Nationale, 1995), p. 121.

22 For example, Organisation for Economic Co-operation and Development, *Quality in Teaching* (Paris: OECD, 1994); OECD, *Measuring the Quality of Schools* (Paris: OECD, 1995); OECD, *Measuring What Students Learn* (Paris: OECD, 1995); OECD, *Education at a Glance: OECD Indicators* (Paris: OECD, 1995).

23 Reynolds and Farrell, *Worlds Apart?*, p. 54.

24 Reynolds and Teddlie, *World Class Schools*; Creemers *et al.*, 'World class schools: some further findings'.

25 W. Keys, 'Take care when you compare', *Times Educational Supplement* (14 June 1996).

26 OECD, *Education at a Glance: OECD Indicators* (Paris: OECD, 1995).

27 Department of Education and Science, *Primary Education in England: A Survey by HM Inspectors of Schools* (London: HMSO, 1978); S.N. Bennett, C. Desforges, A. Cockburn and B. Wilkinson, *The Quality of Pupil Learning Experiences* (Hove: Lawrence Erlbaum, 1984); R.J. Alexander, *Policy and Practice in Primary Education* (London: Routledge, 1997); Alexander *et al.*, *Curriculum Organisation and Classroom Practice in Primary Schools*.

28 Creemers *et al.*, 'World class schools: some further findings'.

29 Reynolds and Teddlie, *World Class Schools*.

30 B. Simon, *The State and Educational Change* (London: Lawrence and Wishart, 1994).

31 R.J. Alexander, *Primary Teaching* (London: Cassell, 1984), pp. 114–30.

32 Benavot *et al.*, 'Knowledge for the masses'.

33 Department of Education and Science, *Primary Education in England*.

34 B.V. Rosenshine, 'Content, time and direct instruction' in P.L. Peterson and H.J. Walberg (eds), *Research on Teaching: Concepts, Findings and Implications* (Berkeley, Calif.: McCutchan, 1979), p. 38.

35 R.J. Alexander, *Versions of Primary Education* (London: Routledge, 1995), pp. 220–69.

36 M. Galton, B. Simon and P. Croll, *Inside the Primary Classroom* (London: Routledge & Kegan Paul, 1980).

37 Alexander, *Policy and Practice in Primary Education*.

38 Broadfoot and Osborn, *Perceptions of Teaching*; M. Osborn and P. Broadfoot, 'A lesson in progress? Primary classrooms observed in England and France' in A. Corbett and R. Moon, *Education in France: Continuity and Change in the Mitterrand Years, 1981–1995* (London: Routledge, 1996).

39 Department of Education and Science, *Aspects of Primary Education in France* (London: DES, 1991); Ofsted, *Aspects of Primary Education in Italy* (London: HMSO, 1994).

40 Alexander *et al., Curriculum Organisation and Classroom Practice in Primary Schools*, p. 10.

7

Leading and managing primary schools: the changing world of the local education authority

Tim Brighouse

This chapter will argue that a period of turbulent and perpetual change in primary education is now giving way to one of confident progress that will be marked by what subsequent generations will see as astonishing advances in educational standards in the primary phase. Indeed, the analysis of this chapter seeks to dispel the uncertainty which still prevails.

But that is to anticipate. First, to origins. The Hadow reports of the 1920s and 1930s, one on secondary and one on primary education, marked the creation in the inter-war years of a separate primary phase.[1] In this sense, of course, the elementary school of the late nineteenth century was the forerunner whose clear but undifferentiated mission was gradually adjusted by successive raises in the age limit for compulsory schooling so that eventually some came to be known as all-age schools. In the years around 1900 Her Majesty's Inspectorate (HMI) reports – towards the end of the first period of payment by results – made the first references to distinctive practice in the early years.[2] Indeed, the London School Board often received reports of outstanding work with infants. Respected and influential pioneers in educational theory as well as practice are immortalized in the names of colleges and schools from the same period (among them Rachel Macmillan, Friedrich Froebel, Maria Montessori).

From Hadow, however, through Plowden, right up to the time of the Black Papers and the William Tyndale affair in Islington in the early 1970s, primary education enjoyed what might be termed a following wind.[3] Never mind that any overall judgement of quality and effectiveness inevitably masked sharply differing practice, the popular mythology encouraged by Plowden and Hadow was of a new breed of primary teachers brought up on the psychological theory of Piaget, effortlessly practising 'progressive' methods. These methods certainly included what have since been criticized as 'child-centred' approaches – what else in fairness, one might ask, should be the centre of teaching activity? – which are characterized as pupils being encouraged to learn when ready to do so and in an environment which encourages them to take charge of their own learning. The pupil in this model becomes a mini-researcher capable of constructing an enquiry, seeking and sifting evidence and writing up and illustrating conclusions. Put like that, and under the guidance of skilled teachers who are quick to spot learning opportunities and changes in the pupils they teach, the model sounds and is ideal. All too often, however, the characterization was represented as caricature both in the account and in reality. Children were or were not ready for 'reading': they engaged in play and their teachers lacked the intellectual cutting edge to do more than occupy them with a busy round of fairly low-level and unfocused activities.

Neither the characterization nor the caricature was widespread, as any survey both of individual HMI reports of the time and of the evidence to Plowden and earlier to Hadow will testify. Much more pervasive was whole-class teaching, rote learning and conservative information-led practice – especially in urban areas, where the bulk of the children were, and still are, educated.

Most of the so-called 'progressive' practice was to be found in county authorities. There, for example, mixed-age classes were not a choice; they were inevitable. Even in the county areas, however, most schools set children in serried ranks and concentrated generation after generation on the three Rs and a limited set of memory games, which was partly reassuring to successive generations of parents. It was not really until I joined Oxfordshire in 1978 that I came across a distinctive and different inheritance and one that might equate to the Piaget–Plowden model.

In Oxfordshire Edith Moorhouse, an adviser and earlier Assistant Education Officer, had formed an alliance with a remarkable member of HMI, Robin Tanner, in the late 1940s and during the 1950s and 1960s. They had an agenda which included overcoming the isolation of often unqualified village school head teachers, which they could see had resulted in a mind-numbing propensity to occupy children in intellectually limited and repetitive tasks. For Moorhouse it was a case of using a battered car for carrying materials and ideas to schools and ferrying heads and teachers to meetings in Cotswold market towns to exchange ideas. For Tanner it was a certainty about good practice that included the development of a child's artistic technique as an essential ingredient. For the primary teachers of Oxfordshire it was the invigorating and affirming – if sometimes intoxicating – realization that they were the focus of external and often international attention. Visitors from the United States and from Sweden were frequent. In the years after Moorhouse in the late 1960s and during the 1970s her successor, John Coe, spread the model into ever widening circles of identifiably similar and (by inference) 'good' practice. By this time some of the practitioners had fallen into unquestioning adherence to the models. This was parodied in asides from critical practitioners from elsewhere as visiting Oxfordshire to see 'triple-mounted' wall displays of children's work which often surrounded a centre-piece of a still life at the heart of which was the obligatory teasel. Like all parodies it contained a connection with reality.

What was interesting about this Oxfordshire adventure in the post-war years was that it was atypical. Mostly authorities ignored what was going on in primary schools. They were too busy managing quantity. More schools needed to be built for the growing populations of new or expanded towns. Worn-out schools needed to be replaced. They also required much logistical managerial expertise and arguments with the Department of Education and Science to secure loan consent for building programmes. After the abandonment for the quota for teachers in the early 1970s, local education authorities (LEAs) were keen to increase the supply of teachers and reduce class size from 50 towards 30. The accent in this age of benign neglect was on quantity not quality.

So Oxfordshire's interest in the quality of what went on in the schools, the fact that, through the advisory service, they had a definitive view of what should go on, was very unusual.

It is, however, true that the theoretical pressure of Piaget in the matter of training and the assiduous work of advisers through in-service courses meant that the influence of what started in Oxfordshire and a few other authorities began to spread. In particular, classroom pedagogical practice moved towards either 'individual monitoring' or 'group teaching' and away from whole-class teaching. From the mid-1970s first Bennett, then Galton and finally Alexander unintentionally supplied, through their research into such teaching methods, the ammunition which was to usher in a reign of terror for primary schools and teachers that began in 1988 with the introduction of the National Curriculum and testing and is likely to last until 1998 with the completion of the first round of primary inspections by the Office for Standards in Education (Ofsted).[4]

Before highlighting the features of the decade of primary terror and looking beyond it to the age of confidence and achievement, I should like to reflect on other features of the age of benign neglect which are significant and demand notice. First, those who ran the education service, whether at a national level or more seriously in the local education authority, boasted teaching experience which was almost without exception at the secondary and not the primary level. So LEA administrators were secondary-influenced. So too were the advisers and the inspectors. The reason is not hard to find. Both administrators and advisers were expected to have degrees – in the immediate post-war years, preferably from Oxford and Cambridge. Of course there were exceptions. For example, for 'organizers' – note, not advisers – of PE or cookery, because these subjects were known to be important for those in the newly created secondary modern schools, candidates could be non-graduates. Early in the century HMI had commented unfavourably on some of the inspectors of local authorities because they were not graduates and by inference uneducated and unworthy of their task.[5]

Contributing to this unpromising state of affairs was the reality that until the 1960s and 1970s and the creation and widespread promotion of the Bachelor of Education degree teachers in primary schools were certified mainly as a result of one- or two-year courses. Graduates they were not. So what chance had those with outstanding talent, intellect and practice to be heard? It is not unfair to say also that in that period of benign neglect the bias towards employing men as head teachers meant that many weak male candidates became leaders of primary schools.

That the period from 1988 has been one of uncertainty and fear bordering on terror cannot seriously be doubted. Consider, first, the impact of the National Curriculum. Until Kenneth Baker insisted otherwise, the oft-reputed conventional wisdom of HMI, psychological theorists, LEA advisers and practitioners in schools was that the primary curriculum was not susceptible to definition solely in terms of subjects. Indeed, by inference 'subjects' as such were not thought of as a suitable framework for an analysis of the primary curriculum at all. Both the Hadow and Plowden reports had given approving illustrations of primary children engaged in research projects on issues arising either from their local environment, current affairs or from a study of some historical event. These illustrations spawned what came to be known as the 'topic' – interestingly, a word used neither in Hadow nor in Plowden but subsequently associated with both.

The National Curriculum, however, determined that the primary curriculum would be defined in terms of the three core and six of the seven foundation subjects (modern languages being an exception) plus, of course, religious education. In disbelief primary teachers received 'cascade' training to familiarize them with a whole new language of attainment targets, standard assessment tasks, key stages and levels.

It is remarkable that such a legislated change should be so efficiently managed. Strangely – for they had in the main opposed the detail both of the curriculum and the assessment design – the LEAs were the management key to the achievement of the new order. It was LEAs, through an increased advisory service, which managed the introduction of the new curriculum and assessment arrangements between 1988 and 1992.

The voices which spoke out during that period, claiming both that the assessment design was too elaborate and inappropriate and that the overall scope and detail of the curriculum as it affected the primary years was too great and therefore impractical to implement, were not LEA voices. They came from the teachers' unions and from academics.

Coinciding with the indigestible change in the curriculum in the primary classroom, the LEAs also ushered in a major managerial and financial upheaval. It was the implementation of the provision within the 1988 Act for local management of schools (LMS). Once again it is astonishing to see how quickly LEAs changed their tune.

Prior to LMS many LEAs determined not just exactly how many teachers and support staff should be in any primary school, but also the amount to be spent on each in a long list of consumable items such as books, cleaning equipment, lavatory rolls and even the telephones, as well as of course as determining priorities among items of repair and maintenance for each school. Indeed, one LEA revealed both its weakness and its strength as a manager of schools by querying the phone bill of a head teacher, bringing in a verdict of not proven and removing the telephone from his office, but leaving him in post and asking him to use the one in the kitchen instead! The very same LEA a few years later claimed to be at the forefront and to have pioneered local management!

How bewildering it must have been for head teachers in some LEAs at the beginning of this period of change, uncertainty and fear. At one moment they had been encouraged, or at least allowed, to assert that they were the professional leaders of the school, leaving the management to a local administration at some distance from the school. At the next they were likened to chief executives and managers and required not merely to master the complexities and bureaucracy of the National Curriculum and testing, but also the computerized intricacies of financial accounting to LEAs for their new-found freedom under LMS.

The shift from change and uncertainty into fear began to emerge clearly in 1992. Up to then LEAs had increased their inspectorates, especially on the primary side, in response both to the necessity of managing the introduction of the National Curriculum and assessment arrangements and to the advice of the Audit Commission which urged them in response to 'losing an empire' to acquire a role in inspection. The Schools Act (1992) changed all that. It ushered in a four-year inspection cycle under the newly created Office for Standards in Education. The cost of the LEA inspection work was estimated and the moneys recovered from local authorities by deductions to the Revenue Support Grant distributed by central government. To survive, LEA advisory services would have to win Ofsted inspection contracts and follow the rubric of the prescribed handbook for its inspection. LEAs had to choose. Many have chosen to inspect their own schools and have run the risk of ruining their relationship of provider, critical friend and improver by being forced either to publish the unvarnished truth to a wide public audience – indeed, some LEAs have pronounced their own schools to be failing! – or to collude in publishing accounts which would reinforce complacency. Other LEAs have chosen to inspect outside their authority. They too have run a risk. For if the financial arrangements for the base funding of the advisory or inspection services have been such that all the time of their inspectors/advisers has been taken up in outside inspection contracts, they have lost touch with the schools and the rationale for their existence.

A few LEAs have been able to steer a middle course by inspecting some schools outside and still leaving sufficient time to support school improvement within the LEA. Pressures on LEA budgets, however, have made that difficult to sustain as a strategy. During a period of such turbulence the capacity of the LEA to monitor changes in the health and well-being of individual schools has never been so important. This is particularly so in urban environments where a drive towards raised standards of educational achievement often seems to take place against an incoming tide of apathy or antagonism bred on ignorance and despair. Schools on their own, as HMI have said, cannot succeed in such circumstances for long.[6] The only agency, however, which can be relied upon to give critical support and intervene in a timely fashion to keep the school on course is the LEA. The key phrase there is 'relied upon'. Clearly chance may mean that an individual school has a relationship with a university or a private consultancy to give it support. But some schools are not looking for support: indeed, they have succumbed to the dangerous belief that they are doing all that can be done. Sometimes, too, governors lack the expertise to penetrate the reality of such a dangerous state of affairs.

But I anticipate the third part of this chapter, which will be to plan to succeed the reign of terror in primary education with one of study, inexorable progress in school improvement and raised standards of educational achievement in the primary phase.

First, however, it is necessary to endure the end of the period of change, uncertainty and fear by completing the first full cycle of four-yearly inspections. While we wait for this to happen, it is inevitable that some more damage will be inflicted in the process on particular schools. The quality of the inspection teams is so uneven that some schools which should be the subject of concern escape serious criticism while others, already moving upwards from a poor base, are set back by inspection teams which are (inevitably) unaware of the school's previous history. As inspectors were wont to say: 'We can only report on what we see at the time'. LEA inspectors, however, gave every impression of being impartial, whereas some private inspection teams appeared to acquire the mantle of hostile witnesses. In any case, the nature of the inevitable snapshot, together with the reference to national norms, seems to be an endemic weakness of the process, compounded, as implied above, by the unevenness of the quality of various Ofsted teams. Quite what is achieved by the public humiliation of being branded a failing school is not immediately clear. Certainly it becomes impossible to tell any member of the parental public who is concerned to exercise his or her preference, that you would send your own child to the school in question! So a dip in intake and the accompanying financial difficulties associated with that is bound to set a publicly failing school backwards still further.

In the years of change, uncertainty and fear, primary teachers and their head teachers have had their confidence and self-esteem challenged at every turn. It was not merely the report of the so-called 'three wise men' in December 1992 which represented the commencement of an open season for public criticism of primary pedagogy.[7] It has been the absence of a cool LEA voice to counterbalance ill-informed media speculation about primary practice. It has also been the appointment of a senior Chief Inspector, Chris Woodhead, whose views of primary practitioners seemed to be more overtly critical, even polemical, than those of his predecessors. For the majority of primary teachers the situation has become almost intolerable. In the budget of 1995 measures were included to set up centres for promoting better primary practice – a theoretical perspective which was itself questioned as an absolute by the three respected classroom researchers, Galton, Bennett and Alexander *et al.*[8]

Certainly the period has witnessed an unparalleled rise in the numbers of primary teachers leaving the profession early, either voluntarily through early retirement or through ill health. Those monitoring and researching the incidence of vacancies in primary headships and deputy headships report increased difficulty in attracting candidates for advertised posts. Why, therefore, is there room for optimism in the matter of the LEA leadership and management of the primary sector? There are four principal reasons.

First, there are signs that the leadership in LEAs themselves is much more informed about primary practice than it was in earlier periods. The graduates with primary experiences are coming through to positions of chief adviser, chief inspector and, significantly, chief education officer as well. There is a world of difference between the discourse I experienced as a young administrator fascinated by primary practice, but alone in speculating about it in an LEA, and that now common in most LEA circles. Second, in the schools themselves the balance of male to female head teachers is in the process of reversing itself. Once again the number of able, strong, sensitive and professionally well-informed female head teachers has increased disproportionately since 1992. The quality of these leaders gives much room for hope. Anecdotal evidence is notoriously unreliable, but it is interesting that the head teachers, both male as it happens, of two remarkably successful and large inner-city Birmingham schools, agree that it is the driving force and energy of able – 'bolshie but positive' – women in their senior management teams which has been the key factor in the improvements in their otherwise very differently run and challenging schools. Third, there is hope that some LEAs are beginning to provide examples of primary leadership by creating a distinctive and different agenda for improvements in primary practice from the failed agenda of the national government. Fourth, and connected, there is the hope that there will be a change in the national agenda in consequence.

It is to these two latter issues that this chapter will finally turn. In the meantime it is essential to make a plea for what academics would call a paradigm shift in the way both primary issues and primary management are considered. I refer to differentiation.

From Hadow to the present day, writings and reports from primary education have suffered from the very failing which those who have written the reports in recent years have themselves levelled at teachers – a lack of differentiation. It is simply not good enough to talk of primary education as though it is the same thing across the UK as a whole. It is not.

In Oxfordshire, where I worked for a decade, a small school was 30 pupils; in Birmingham, where I now work, it is 210 pupils. In Oxfordshire a very large school was 400; this is unremarkable in Birmingham, where a large school is 750. Just because politicians have undermined their intentions by wishing the same prescriptions on all schools, there is no need for writers, academics and practitioners alike to fall into the same trap of generalization.

Birmingham is different from Oxford, and London is different again. London, for example, has a high teacher turnover – a fatal wound for the education of young children in urban areas – while Birmingham does not. Teachers live and work in our city, and it gives us a tremendous advantage.

But it is more serious than that. Birmingham schools are so different from one another. Perhaps you know enough about the city to guess that schools in the Royal Borough of Sutton Coldfield are different from those in Handsworth or Aston and Newtown. But again, schools in Aston and Newtown are often very different from one another.

One of the solutions to the challenge of differentiation would be to create a standing national task force on primary education. It could perhaps be a Select Committee of the House of Commons with additional external membership, and would be charged with considering and dispensing funds targeted at the margin to raise standards in named LEAs with features which we can loosely describe as typical of urban or rural disadvantage. Each LEA in turn would be matched with two others showing broadly similar characteristics – whether of ethnicity, poverty or educational outcome – and all these would be expected to share examples of information, research, professional development and practice with the express intention of learning, one from another. Within each of the authorities schools would be similarly brought into families and given similar sets of purposes.

Given differentiation of management practice, there are two main reasons for assuming we can witness a remarkable rise in standards of educational achievement as LEAs shift their focus in order to embrace school improvement alongside their role in providing services, acting as an arbiter in matters of individual rights and planning new or the removal of old provision.

First, there is the certainty we now have that high-quality pre-school provision pays off in the teenage years and beyond, with lower bills for special programmes for those who hitherto have been casualties of the system. Moreover, it is urgent that we do not confine such programmes to mean simply a part-time place in nursery school or class for all 3-year-olds. In urban areas it must also encompass a targeted cohesive package of policies and practices affecting housing, health and education for first-time single mothers – especially those in disadvantaged circumstances. One simple reform which would have a long-term pay-off would be to reserve health visitor support for such unsupported first-time mothers and to widen the health visitor's brief to incorporate an overtly educational agenda.

There are now sufficient examples of inter-agency working for the government to spell out a range of options and to stipulate the adoption of at least one by the various departments of the local authorities, the health authorities and the voluntary sector. Planning and management from a single agency are essential.

The second main reason for optimism is the school improvement knowledge now available to LEAs. If this is acted upon, it is now possible to look forward to uninterrupted progress in primary standards of academic achievement. Consider the Birmingham example.

We start, as elsewhere, with the shifting balance towards better female leadership and the quality of provision that improves with each cohort of new recruits, both at the newly qualified teacher level and in the leadership of schools.

To that we have added an analysis of the processes of school improvement which are derived from a review of the characteristics of school effectiveness research. So we believe it possible to go beyond the lists of characteristics enumerated by various researchers into the primary field such as Barbara Tizard and Peter Mortimore, as well, of course, as the many pamphlets supplied by HMI and Ofsted.[9] We have promoted shared knowledge of a map of school improvement, including seven processes necessarily encountered by schools on a daily basis. These seven processes are:

- *The exercise of leadership*. This is to be encountered at all levels within the school and involves the Deputy Head, all those holding particular posts of responsibility, all staff, pupils, governors and others in the sharing of responsibility. The head teacher becomes the guardian of the school's vision rather than its only provider. The sharing of leadership is a regular item for discussion in successful primary schools.

- *The practice of management.* Whether in the arrangements of meetings, the ordering of materials, the provision of reports, the organization of parents' evenings and other consultations, or in the discharge of successful learning and teaching, the school is always engaged in the management process. Management is 'getting the detail right'. The success or otherwise of management is most affected by size of organization. Frequently, over-complex school management has the capacity to smother a school. Procedures appropriate in a large organization are not so in a small one and the school is a combination of both.

- *The creation of an environment fit for learning.* Each day all members of a school community affect their own environment by their behaviour towards one another. Primary schools are probably well known for using the visual environment in all sorts of subtle ways, both inside and outside, to reinforce the learning. Aurally, too, a school's environment can be a force or not for learning. Carpets, for example, are now seen as commonplace aids to the classroom teacher's efforts to find the optimum number of moments to surprise children into learning or understanding things they never thought within their scope. Music, too, is increasingly used to affect mood – even to increase the success of language teaching. Finally, behaviour policies affect the environment. The elusive ethos of the school is to be found in the habits of personal dealing, whether adult with adult, or adult with child, or child with child.

- *The practice of collective review.* Perhaps the most important of processes is collective review, which of course a school can ignore if it wishes, but at a high price. Collective review is that simple process whereby groups of staff – and sometimes governors and parents, too – review existing policies. So, for example, what are the aims of a school's practices in reading within its language policy? What are its present practices in this respect? What other practices are possible – either previously experienced by members of the school community or known to be effective elsewhere? What evidence is collected to judge the effectiveness of existing practice and alternatives known? What does it tell the school? How should the school proceed in the future? Out of such regular review of different aspects of a primary school comes a greater shared ownership and a constant improvement to the stock of intellectual curiosity and capital of the school.

- *The practice of staff development.* This is not merely in-service opportunities. It is the way advertisements and job descriptions are written by the school. It includes induction and membership of committees or working group opportunities, personal and professional individual plans for all, not simply teaching staff. Where staff development is successful there are few staff absences. Staff members talk about teaching;

they plan their work together, they have opportunities to observe each other teach and help the learning process with a common agenda outside the appraisal system. Teachers and support staff engage in teaching each other new skills and presenting new ideas as a matter of course.

- *The involvement of the parents and the rest of the community.* Not so long ago notices such as 'No parents beyond this point' decorated the top of broken glass bedecked school walls. We have come a long way since those days, although there is a paradox in the respective roles of parents as consumers and parents as joint educators. Both demand, however, that a school provide ample information to a variety of parents – even when to do so risks criticism. Many schools, knowing that children are in the care of their parents and the rest of the community for 85 per cent of their waking life, with only the 15 per cent balance being at school, are reviewing their approach to parental partnership. For these schools some year groups start with a parent–teacher–child consultation which leads to the three agreeing targets for learning for the year, shared experiences and an explicit agreement to relative rights and responsibilities which will lead to a mid-year review of progress made and new goals set.
- *The practice of learning and teaching.* A successful school recognizes that it is always reviewing its central activity with a view to learning more about it. The learning is promoted for all members of the school community, not simply the pupils, so that they are surrounded by good role models. Staff meetings are on a rota to be hosted in different classrooms by different members of staff who explain their practice as a first item on the staff meeting agenda. Such meetings are therefore geared towards debate about teaching and learning. The head and deputy are seen to be joining in and sometimes leading debate about teaching and learning.

There is of course a multitude of practice to share about each of these seven processes – as well as the findings of research. The point is that for the first time schools are being encouraged to share practice through the creation of a common language and a map of school improvement. It is for them, however, to think about practice. The LEA cannot and should not do that for them, because the contexts of schools are so very different.

The LEA, however, can go beyond simply setting out the processes and map of school improvement. It can seek to set a climate within which schools might have a better chance of improving. An obvious example is, of course, the provision of money. Better budgets improve morale and increase the opportunity for schools to try out new ideas, replenish libraries and improve facilities. In Birmingham we have gone far beyond that. We have sought to affect climate in two ways. First, we have endeavoured to enlist the support of the whole community by establishing a series of 'Years of . . .'. The first was primary education, the next reading, the third IT. The fourth will be numeracy, followed by the arts and so on. In each year, which is telegraphed well in advance so that schools can take advantage of their development planning of a city-wide emphasis on one particular aspect of learning; a group of enthusiasts plans and orchestrates activities. These include celebration, in-service training, parental education, the involvement of the business community and an emphasis to affect all in the service, whether teachers, governors or parents.

Second, we have dared to create a 'Primary Guarantee' which sets out three targets of input, five targets of experience and, crucially, two of outcome.

The targets of input are designed to keep LEA managers and politicians up to the mark. There is a commitment to protect the primary budget and to seek to improve it in real terms year after year. Managers are pledged to guarantee levels of services to schools and the LEA promises to organize periodic inputs from national and international experts on school improvement.

The targets of experience – emphasizing a residential experience, the arts, public performance, writing and an environmental project for all youngsters – are meant to signpost symbolically important points that might have been lost in the detail of the National Curriculum.

It is, however, in the two targets of outcome that the Primary Guarantee breaks really new ground. The targets relate to literacy – especially reading – and numeracy levels at age 7 and age 11. Using a bank of statements drawn from the National Curriculum assessment levels, but adding to them and renaming them to fit in with what we know about successful practice, schools are invited to set targets each with a higher variant for each successive cohort. From this progress it is hoped that city targets for improved standards will emerge. In each school the process should encourage target-setting for children – preferably involving the parents and as suggested earlier in this chapter. The expected outcome is a climatic shift in expectation.

Of course, the LEA does much more to underpin this new programme for primary schools. There is a need to look after all staff and to provide examples both of valuing people publicly while in private taking action against those few who are letting down the children of the city. In order not to fool ourselves we are taking light samples of 9-year-olds' standards in maths and English. We need to get right our approach to bilingualism and our partnership with the many communities which combined to provide Birmingham with its multi-ethnic and multi-faceted mix.

To this potent mix of more highly qualified and skilful staff and a clearer focus by management on qualitative improvement, one can now add the evident promise of information technology. In the primary sector, in particular, one can begin to see the potential – equivalent to the arrival of the printed book – it now offers to pupil achievement and teacher expertise.

So in this prospective new period the agenda is for a new phase in primary education. It assumes confidence and growing success. Perhaps it is a period in which primary schools will at last have come of age. Self-reviewing with critical external advice, we should be on a path of ever higher standards of educational achievement, working closely with parents to secure that critical tuning of expectation that leads to self-esteem which on a daily basis can bring such confidence to children who never learn as easily again as they do in the years before adolescence. Notwithstanding poverty, and especially home circumstances, many of us have already witnessed what remarkable teachers and support staff in schools in the primary sector can do in the urban context where, as we have remarked earlier, the real battle for educational success will be won or lost. The stage is now set for those examples to become the norm.

Notes

1 Ministry of Education, *Hadow Reports*, reports on the Consultative Committee (London: HMSO, 1926, 1931, 1933).
2 Department of Education and Science, *A Survey of the Quality of 4-Year-Olds in Primary Classes: Report by HMI* (London: HMSO, 1989).
3 Central Advisory Council for Education (CACE), *Children and Their Primary Schools* (London: HMSO, 1967); C. Cox and A. Dyson (eds), *Fight for Education: A Black Paper* (Manchester: Critical Quarterly Society, 1969); see J. Gretton, *William Tynedale: Collapse of a School or a System?* (London: George Allen & Unwin, 1976).
4 N. Bennett, *Teaching Styles and Pupil Progress* (London: Open Books, 1976); M. Galton, B. Simon and P. Croft, *Inside the Primary Classroom* (London: Routledge & Kegan Paul, 1980); R. Alexander, J. Rose and C. Woodhead, *Curriculum Organization and Classroom Practice in Primary Schools* (London: HMSO, 1992).
5 See J. Hurt, 'Parental involvement in schools' in C. Cullingford (ed.), *Parents, Teachers and Schools* (London: Royce, 1985), pp. 17–40.
6 Alexander *et al.*, *Curriculum Organization and Classroom Practice in Primary Schools*.
7 Alexander *et al.*, *Curriculum Organization and Classroom Practice in Primary Schools*.
8 Galton *et al.*, *Inside the Primary Classroom*; Bennett, *Teaching Styles and Pupil Progress*; Alexander *et al.*, *Curriculum Organization and Classroom Practice in Primary Schools*.
9 B. Tizard and M. Hughes, *Young Children Learning* (London: Fontana, 1984); P. Mortimore, P. Sammons, L. Stoll, D. Lewis and R. Ecob, *School Matters: The Junior Years* (London: Open Books, 1988).

8

Governors, parents and primary schools

Felicity Taylor

Introduction

When I attended my first Primary Education Study Group (PESG) meeting in 1987, which was on the theme 'Primary Education Matters', there were two contributions on the role of school governors. One was from Bill Percival himself, entitled, ominously, 'Opening Pandora's box: primary education and parents'.[1] He foresaw a number of problems arising from the new powers given to parents and governors:

- Lack of a framework: no general understanding or agreement about the place of parents in their relationship with the educators.
- The need for models for developing successful strategies for involving parents in three roles: as governors, as consumers and as educators.
- Modes of dialogue between more fluent and more confident teachers and parents.
- Opening the curriculum and the clash of values: 'The debate will not be clearly defined, coherent and on a national scale'.
- The cost – in terms not in money but in teacher stress because of the need for new skills and the ability to live with ambiguity, compromise and negotiation. Teachers will need the support of an equally hard-thinking, committed and resilient parent constituency. ('If we fail to get both we will be in deep trouble'.)

The other contribution was from Anne Sofer, some time before she became a chief education officer. Discussing the 1986 Education Act, she referred to the atmosphere of conflict in which education was being conducted, and to the increasing tendency for both sides in the conflict to enroll parents as (willing or unwilling) supporters of their cause. (She also suggested that the challenge for local authorities would be to refrain from swaddling governors in more bureaucracy, a challenge that, alas, some of them have failed to meet.) She predicted that school governorship could become one of the most important instruments of adult political education, an important and unique model of grassroots political participation. How many parent governors, she wondered, would become involved in politics proper?

What has happened since those perspicacious PESG comments in 1987?

Lack of a framework

A great deal of legislation since 1987 has aimed to establish parents in a central role in the education service. The Parent's Charter draws together in one document parents' rights, responsibilities and choices in education.[2] The most detailed and specific of these is the right to know. Parents have a right to a substantial and often daunting file of information about their own and other local schools (see Table 8.1). Unfortunately much of this information is not very accessible to parents, especially those for whom English is a second language. Schools are trying harder to communicate with parents – many primary schools would not even have had a prospectus ten years ago and competitions like *The Times Educational Supplement* prize for the best annual report set a good example.

Other new rights mentioned in the Charter include the right of access to a formal procedure for complaints about the curriculum, though not necessarily about other aspects of school life, and a mandatory procedure for exclusion from school. It may be significant, however, that in spite of all the talk of partnership, there is still no statutory right to have a home–school association or PTA, nor for parents to have access to the classroom, though they do now have, in primary as well as secondary and special schools, the right to an annual written report on their child.

The need for models of development: how successful have we been in involving parents in their three roles?

Parents as governors

The changes in the composition of governing bodies brought about by the 1986 Education Act had a dramatic and largely beneficial effect on the average governing body. Parent governors found more safety in numbers and grew in confidence. They also formed alliances with the teacher

Table 8.1 Information for parents

Governors must:
- publish a school prospectus containing statutory information;
- publish an annual report to parents with required information;
- ensure that the school makes required documents available to parents:
  - any statutory instruments, circulars and administrative memoranda relating to the curriculum
  - any published Ofsted reports on the school
  - all schemes of work and syllabuses used in the school
  - the arrangements about making complaints
  - information about religious education
  - the school prospectus
  - the Annual Report to Parents;
- in secondary schools, include in the annual report or publish a supplementary document giving details of public exam results, with national and local comparative tables; also the school's aggregated results of SATs at KS3;
- in primary schools, distribute the comparative tables of exam results to parents of children transferring to secondary school; include the school's aggregated results of SATs at KS1 and 2 in the annual report;
- see that the agendas, minutes and accompanying reports (except for confidential items) for governors' meetings are on display in the school;
- publish the special needs policy in the prospectus and report on its operation in school;
- ensure that records and reports are kept according to DfEE regulations.

Source: Institute of School and College Governors, *Handbook for School Governors* (London: ISCG, 1994)

governors. Here were people who had a direct and very pressing personal interest in what was going on in their school. They could not afford to take a long-run view, because in the long run their children would be somewhere else. Even so, they could become a force for change and improvement.

The recruitment of parent governors has improved steadily, although it is still patchy. There are inner-city schools with a high proportion of parents for whom English is a second language and who, despite the linguistic complication, provide excellent models for involving parents. There are other schools, many in more affluent areas, who may have abandoned the classic 'No parents beyond this point' notice in material form but still have it written in their hearts. Parents are not slow to pick up these hidden messages.

Parents as governors do have problems. They cannot possibly claim to speak for all parents, and they often feel that they have a hostage to the school in the shape of their own child. It is not easy to achieve the right balance between using the insider knowledge that a parent has, and generalizing too much from the experience of one's own child. It is not uncommon to hear head teachers complain that parent governors fail to recognize that they have wider responsibilities than to their own children.

Although parent governors may be able to act as mediators in difficult situations, other parents sometimes expect too much from them – 'You're a governor, why don't you do something?' – not realizing that they have no specific powers to take action. They are also often expected to shoulder all the responsibility for communication between the governing body and parents. Other governors should also make it their business to ascertain what parents think.

Parents as consumers

Government strategy to encourage parents as consumers centres on the rhetoric of choice. Clued-up parents, they have argued, armed with league tables and school prospectuses, will make informed choices of school for their children and so market forces will improve standards. Unfortunately, a free market depends on elasticity of supply and popular schools stretch their elasticity to the limit. It should have been obvious from the start that, for instance, it is impossible for the infant school with one-form entry on a restricted site to expand to take all comers – let alone that the reason for its popularity may well be its small size and intimacy. What can be claimed for the legislation on admissions is that it has reduced the opportunities for heads to pick and choose their clientele, at least in schools maintained by local education authorities (LEAs).

Still proceeding on market assumptions, the government laid it down that the governing body must hold a meeting for parents modelled on an annual shareholders' meeting, at which they present their annual report to parents. This is intended to be a review of the year's work, at which the parents can call the governors and the school to account.

It is no secret that some governing bodies resent spending time and effort on the annual parents' meeting, because, they say, few parents bother to turn up or even to read the report. Other governing bodies use the occasion to celebrate the life and work of their school with staff and parents. This seems to be more successful in persuading parents to attend.

The unpopularity of the annual parents' meeting probably originated in the way the event was mistakenly presented to parents, as a chance to get back at the school. Most parents feel reasonably happy with their children's education and do not relish an evening spent castigating the school in public, or listening to others doing so. This is borne out by the way in which the Office for Standards in Education (Ofsted) meetings and questionnaire to parents almost always, even in difficult schools, produce very positive comments about the school. 'It's our school, you leave us alone' might sum up the prevailing feelings. The wry comment that the way to make a school popular is to threaten to close it has manifest evidence to support it.

One area where concerns of parents have had an effect can be seen in the willingness on the part of schools to take more seriously anxieties and complaints about bullying and racial harassment. All too often these used to be brushed aside as a natural hazard of school life. Staff are now expected to act and to be seen to act firmly against bullying, and strategies to combat bullying and harassment feature in the school prospectus.

Parents as educators

Research has indicated that working in partnership with parents may be the key to effective education and the majority of schools now perceive parents as a valuable resource. However, other changes in society militate against the trend. Social and economic factors mean that more mothers of primary school children now go out to work, and are not able to contribute as much as they would like to working with the school. More fathers may be unemployed, but there can be some resistance to men helping in primary schools. So while teachers become more eager to involve parents, parents often find it more difficult to respond. It can be frustrating for both parties. Parents, tired and under stress, may be tempted to ask what teachers think they are being paid for. Teachers, tired and under stress, may be tempted to blame the parents for not caring.

Schools can almost always persuade parents to come in to talk about their own children's progress. Perhaps the most exciting trend has been the development of shared assessment with parent, pupil and teacher – a dialogue that benefits and educates all three.

Modes of dialogue

It is still the case that most initial teacher training contains very little about working with parents and governors. Young teachers are more fluent and confident, and conscious that they do possess a high degree of professional skill. The fact that this is not recognized, particularly by some sections of the press, creates an unhelpful climate. Parents have been conditioned by media coverage to be aware that they have rights to influence what goes on in school. Many schools report a rise in the number of complaints from parents, sometimes on quite trivial matters. What is surprising is that this unhelpful combination has not led to a general decline in parent–teacher relations – very much the reverse. Why?

I believe it is because of the dialogue that goes on in the governing body. By setting up a mandatory composition for governing bodies that gave no single group a majority, an environment was created which is intrinsically less threatening both to teachers and to parents. Some head teachers may wish to disagree, but at least they can no longer be faced with a governing body dominated by local councillors, or any other group with its own agenda – or at least it is more difficult for that to happen. In particular, where governing bodies have divided up their roles and responsibilities among committees, especially committees on which staff also serve, the dialogue can become a very creative and motivating factor in school improvement.

Opening the curriculum and the clash of values

It turned out that the clash of values was not so much between parents and teachers as between schools and the government's National Curriculum Council (NCC). Most schools and parents were broadly in favour of the principle of the National Curriculum. It was the detailed prescription that made it unmanageable and forced the Dearing review. Certainly governors found that it gave them a key to the secret garden, even if some skill is needed to turn the key and the garden was subjected to a period of forced growth that eventually needed drastic pruning. One day we may be able to make more considered judgements about the blame for an expensive mistake, but the professional advisers cannot avoid some responsibility for the overload.

Where parents stand on the ideology of the curriculum is not easy to determine. Parents are no more homogeneous in their opinions than teachers or governors, far less homogeneous than politicians. Of course they want their children to read, write and count, but other than that they are generally prepared to trust the teachers if the teachers look as if they know what they are doing, and the school appears to be a happy, ordered place. The three wise men's pronouncements, even in their more distorted versions, did not change this confidence materially.[3] Primary teachers report that parents generally are more interested in looking at their children's carefully selected and labelled portfolio of work, than in discussing the results of Standard Assessment Tasks, though of course they want to know where their children stand in relation to others.

The argument with parents about values that Bill Percival feared has so far failed to materialize except in a few rare cases. Most parents have more instinctive sympathy with the somewhat woolly but benevolent values of the average primary school than with the evangelical certainties of special interest groups. Where such groups have endeavoured to hijack the debate there have been determined and well-informed governors and parents to see them off. In two recent cases of so-called scandals about sex education or sexual orientation it was very noticeable that the governors and parents were much more robust in their defence of the school than the local councillors and officers felt able to be.

That the debate would not be clearly defined or coherent was an easy guess. 'Up to now most of it has been simplistic, rhetorical and anecdotal', said Bill. It still mostly is. One of my complaints, in a brief and ineffective spell as a member of the NCC, was that no attempt was made to engage parents and governors in the important issues. Today's debates, though still superficial, are more national than predicted. The debate on school improvement is a good example. The general consensus on what makes a good school is not couched in professional jargon as once it might have been, but in ways that everyone can understand. No one who works with primary school governors can help but be impressed by their commitment, their knowledge and understanding of the debate on teaching and learning, their capacity to spot cant and fudge.

The cost

Are we in deep trouble? That there has been a substantial cost is certain. Teachers have been demoralized, demotivated and depressed. A large part of the time of the conscientious chair of governors is spent on bolstering the morale of a desperately anxious head and staff. Teaching in the inner city, even in primary schools, often has more to do with containment than education. And yet I strongly believe that, in spite of all the traumas, the education the average child receives in the average primary classroom is better than it was ten years ago. It is more focused, more varied, more professional.

We have also begun to recognize that something has to be done about teachers who are not coping. I am sure that this is because of the influence of parents and teachers on governing bodies and because of governing bodies' responsibility for personnel issues. Bad teachers, especially bad head teachers, do so much damage that they must be removed. But the current emphasis on outright failure is very unfair. It does nothing to help teacher morale or to improve teacher performance. There is no evidence that the dole queues are full to overflowing with great teachers waiting to fill the gaps in the ranks so eagerly demanded by some leading figures who ought to know better.

All teachers need help, support and, above all, time. And that is precisely what is being taken away from them. They have less help and support from advisers, less chance for discussion about good practice with colleagues, less time to reflect. There is nothing new about that, but what is new is that parents and governors who are involved in their schools now appreciate it too and are hard-thinking, committed and resilient enough to fight for it.

Today's parents and governors are sophisticated enough to understand that the factors with a true significance for school improvement have a real cost. It will be interesting to see whether the new government's initiatives are any more successful than that of the current administration in capturing the allegiances of parents and governors. They may well go on saying 'Put your money where your mouth is'.

Whose side are they on?

In the aftermath of the teachers' pay disputes, who in 1987 would have expected that parents, teachers and governors would make common cause against the government on at least three major issues – finance, national tests and class size?

A junior minister of the time once remarked that no constituents ever gave him any grief about teachers' pay. They do now. Handing over control of finance to school governing bodies was an excellent reform in many ways, because it has meant that money is spent more swiftly and effectively to meet individual school needs. But one of the unforeseen side-effects is that many more parents and governors are now aware of what 'financial stringency' means in physical terms – loss of a valued teacher, yet another year in 30-year-old prefabs. What they perceive is no longer the teachers whingeing again, but the tangible disadvantage for their children and their school, and they are becoming more and more determined not to put up with it. So much so that governments find it advisable to claim it has found more money for education, and councils which rob the education budget find themselves beset by angry parent and governor demonstrations.

The débâcle over national testing was perhaps more unexpected. It shows how much parents, governors and teachers were in sympathy and how out of touch were the politicians. What happened was very clear. Governing bodies listened to their teachers and believed what they had to say, because they had been in the classroom and seen for themselves. They had built up a trust and partnership with their staff which they did not want to damage. They were not prepared to use heavy sanctions to force teachers to do something which as professionals they believed was wrong. It was not so much that parents and teachers were on the teachers' side; they were putting the interests of the children first.

The class size argument is a good example of the gulf between the practitioner and the theorist. Theorize as much as you like about the evidence to be adduced from research, your average teacher or parent will not believe you. They will say that it stands to reason that smaller classes mean more attention for each child and less stress on the teacher. Arguments about classes of 50 in 'the old days' or in South-East Asia cut little ice with anyone who has been in a modern primary classroom, computers and all. Small classes may not compensate for poor teaching, but it would be hard to prove that they make it worse.

There is a down side to this. Teachers who are or should be expert communicators ought not to find it difficult to get parents on their side. That does not mean that they are always right, and sometimes decisions may have to be taken that will be unpopular in the staffroom. If one of the functions of the effective governing body is to provide an independent perspective on the life and work of the school, then relationships ought not to be too cosy. That is one reason why it is a disadvantage to have too many parents on a governing body. Schools are insular enough as it is, and need exposure to a wider range of experience.

In fact, the relations between governing bodies and the head teacher and staff naturally include some degree of tension. If they are too relaxed, the governors are probably failing in at least part of their triple role – the strategic view, the critical friend, and the vehicle for accountability. To this extent, Anne Sofer was right in describing governorship as adult political education, though the politics is seldom one of parties.

The world of local politics is not so likely to attract governors as it was ten years ago, when, for example, a number of parent campaigners became members (representing both major parties) of the ILEA, because it did seem then that they could influence the system for the better. The declining powers of the LEA make that a less attractive prospect.

However, if by politics is meant the science of getting things done, changed and improved, then the governing body is the ideal training ground. Tact, diplomacy and determination are just a few of the qualities honed by being a governor. Other skills can also be acquired: working in a team, reaching consensus among differing views, making the best use of scarce resources, planning, monitoring, evaluating, managing groups, writing reports. It is very exciting to watch young parent governors in the primary school find out how much they can improve their experience and knowledge through being governors, as well as their chances of getting a paid job.

While many governors enjoy their new roles, they do not want to be left to cope with every problem themselves. They soon learn that they need and have a right to professional support and advice. Early suspicion of the LEA can lead to politically conscious understanding of its necessary role, as long as the LEA avoids ham-fisted intervention and excessive bureaucracy.

Potential and actual conflicts between head teachers and governors give rise to concern. Many primary heads have been catapulted into a world of school management completely different from when they entered the profession. Head teachers who lack confidence react defensively to criticism, especially when naively or aggressively expressed. Conflicts often arise because heads and governors are operating with different assumptions. The importance of purposeful leadership in running an effective school is rightly stressed. Some heads may be led to confuse strong leadership with dictatorship, to presume that they alone have the professional skills, knowledge and experience to take the right decisions. Meanwhile, the governors have been led to believe that better decisions come from a group of people with an interest in the result, contributing their own knowledge and experience while listening to professional advice.

Some decisions do require flair and vision, an imaginative and possibly risky leap into the unknown. Good head teachers will be able to persuade the governors when this is right. However, most school decisions depend rather on convincing a disparate group of people with many different agendas that a particular course of action is the best one, so that they will be prepared to support it. The leader with charisma has an easy task; but charisma is in short supply. Being prepared to listen so that you can get the best out of everyone may not provide political soundbites, but it is a useful substitute and has the advantage that it is within more people's grasp.

Do governors make a difference?

What effect have these changes had on the average primary school governing body, and on the average primary school? In September 1994 Sir Peter Newsam suggested:

> As the influence of local education authorities dwindles, governors are one of the few remaining obstacles to virtually unfettered state control of education in the UK. In that role governors are far more important now than they have ever been in the past.[4]

If a school is genuinely failing its pupils, governors have a duty to make it their top priority. But this is when the school is in crisis. Most governors are more concerned with helping their school to get better. Their outside perspective on old problems and 'the way we do things here' can act as a a catalyst for improvement. Ideas and strategies can be generated through joint working parties with staff which allow time for reflection and discussion.

Value-added measures or Ofsted itself can show up some unsuspected weaknesses. A governing body which is performing its role of scrutiny and evaluation is a defence against growing stale and resting on one's laurels. It is also a protection for parents and the community against the abuse of power. On the other hand, a governing body which has earned the trust of the head teacher and staff and knows the school's strengths and weaknesses can be a valuable ally and bulwark against unfair attack when the going gets rough.

So of course they can make a difference. Whether or not they do so depends partly on their own energies and skills, and partly on the culture of the school. As Bill Percival warned, partnership does not happen by accident. It has to be worked for. If the school does not respect its governing body and its parents it will not be able to count on their support. And that can be a very lonely position in the harsh world of the 1990s. We need to make sure that we get every scrap of hope out of Pandora's box.

Notes

1 S.W. Percival, 'Opening Pandora's box: primary education and parents', paper presented to the Primary Education Study Group (April 1987).
2 Department for Education and Employment, *The Parent's Charter Updated* (London: HMSO, 1994).
3 R. Alexander, J. Rose and C. Woodhead, *Curriculum Organization and Classroom Practice in Primary Schools* (London: HMSO, 1992).
4 P. Newsam, 'Governor's guide', *Times Educational Supplement* (30 September 1994).

9

Voyages of discovery: changing perspectives in research on primary school practice

Neville Bennett

Introduction

Early in the 1970s I began an intellectual voyage. This was not some eso-
teric quest for the Holy Grail or nirvana, but for the much more practical
purpose of enhancing our understandings of the complexity of primary
practice, with a view to its improvement. It has, like all voyages of discovery, been characterized by both elation and frustration, sometimes
speeding in full empirical sail, and at other times buffeted by high political winds or becalmed in the theoretical doldrums. The voyage has taken
me into uncharted waters and has thus required the drawing of new, or
modified, pedagogical maps or models. My travels have, of course, all
been previously recorded, but rarely in a holistic manner such that the con-
nectedness, coherence and significance of the whole can be ascertained.[1]
This therefore is the purpose of the following account.

Teaching styles

My first foray into research on primary practice began immediately after
the completion of my PhD. This relied on data collected in classrooms but
could hardly be called classroom research. It exemplified educational
research at that time – a highly sophisticated number-crunching exercise
to test, in this instance, hypotheses relating to children's intelligence,

personality and creative attainment. It did, nevertheless, contain the seed for the study of teaching styles which was to flower later. The idea came from the realization that two of the classes I had used in this study were well matched in such characteristics as class size, the mean and range of children's verbal reasoning scores, and social economic background. They had, however, been taught in very different ways, which could crudely be labelled traditional and progressive. In comparing the outcomes of these classes some fascinating trends appeared. The children in the so-called progressive class gained higher scores in creative writing and on measures of motivation. The children in the traditional class, on the other hand, had the advantage in scores on mathematics and language, and were less anxious. Nothing could be made of, or claimed for, these findings; they were simply *ex post facto* reanalyses of test scores in two classes. They did nevertheless tie in with the findings of contemporary psychological studies of creativity, and of the relationships between classroom structure and children's anxiety levels. They also served to raise questions about the validity of the Plowden panacea that 'finding out' was, in all circumstances, and for all intended learning outcomes, better than 'being told'.

It is surprising, in retrospect, that at this time researchers had barely discovered classrooms. There was a burgeoning psychological literature on learning, but virtually nothing on teaching. As such, researchers wishing to gain better understandings of classroom processes had little to guide them. The theories of teaching then available were few, and based not on observations of practice, but loosely on conceptions of democracy, leading to such dichotomies as authoritarian versus democratic teaching. The prescriptive theory advocated by Plowden,[2] which distinguished between progressive and traditional practices, fitted this same mould. It was, like the penny-farthing, crudely and awkwardly fashioned, but the best thing then available.

Our study was typical of those then published, and of those which were to follow, in being characterized by the collection of data on teachers' classroom practices, on which were computed classifications or typologies of teaching styles. Teachers were then chosen who represented these styles, which in our study ranged along a dimension we labelled informal–formal, and their pupils were followed over one school year, in which their attainments, behaviours and personalities were measured at the beginning and the end of the year to assess change.

Our findings from the study of teaching styles were remarkably similar to those of the two earlier case studies. In general, children taught by formal and mixed teaching styles showed greater progress in maths and language, and anxious children behaved and performed better in these classrooms. On the other hand, children in informal classes improved more in motivation, and the best teacher overall was an extremely well-organized informal teacher. The worst teachers also taught informally, although with much less organization and structure.

We also found that the majority of teachers adopted mixed styles, choosing those features of both formal and informal styles which suited their particular beliefs and approach. Two years later, in its 1978 survey of nearly 550 primary schools in England, Her Majesty's Inspectorate (HMI) found even fewer exploratory (its term for informal or progressive) teachers. Most teachers in its survey were at the formal end of the continuum.[3] It, too, reported that children taught by mixed and formal teaching approaches obtained significantly higher score in maths and reading. Later, Maurice Galton and his colleagues reported that the most successful style, in terms of children's attainments, was one they labelled 'classroom enquirers' – a group of teachers who emphasized questioning, and devoted more time than the other styles to class teaching, such that much of the learning was teacher-managed.[4] These findings are typical of studies of teaching style on both sides of the Atlantic.[5]

Few studies of teaching style were undertaken after the 1970s, and this was not merely the result of research whim or fashion. Studies based on this theoretical perspective suffered several difficulties. Because they tended to be based on theories of teaching which were ideologically, rather than empirically, grounded – that is, on an ideology aligned to a particular set of political beliefs about the nature of man and society – they tended to generate more political heat than pedagogical light.[6] A major technical problem was that of definition. Styles were defined as groups or bundles of teacher practices, making it impossible to ascertain the impact of any one aspect of practice, such as grouping, or assessment, or subject teaching, on pupils' achievement, attitudes or motivation. Yet it is the identification of such individual aspects of practice on which effective professional development depends. Another problem was the large between-style differences. For example, although, on average, formal styles related to better progress, some formal teachers were able to generate much better progress than other formal teachers. Similarly, some informal teachers were successful, but others were much less so. In other words, teaching style in itself did not, and could not, provide an adequate explanation of differences in pupil outcomes. Its power as a theory, in allowing understandings and predictions of practice, was therefore extremely limited. It had outlived its usefulness (except, of course, for headline writers). New theories were thus needed which would allow the identification of specific teacher and pupil behaviours, and the links to specified classroom outcomes. But where were these to be found?

Opportunity to learn

The clue came from reflecting back on the observational data collected in the teaching styles study in an attempt to identify what differentiated the more from the less successful teachers, irrespective of their teaching style. We found that the more successful teachers devoted more time to mathematics and language activities, and that a higher proportion of their pupils' time was spent on-task. These findings were congruent with a new perspective being developed at that time around the concept of 'opportunity to learn'. The underlying premise of this was that, other things being equal, pupil achievement was determined by the opportunity provided by teachers for pupils to study given curriculum content, and by the use made of that opportunity by pupils, that is, in terms of their involvement or on-task behaviour.[7] Unlike the teaching styles approach, there is no assumption here that teaching directly affects learning. All effects of teaching are seen to be mediated by pupils' activities. So from this perspective pupils are the central focus, with teachers seen as the managers of attention and time.

The broadest aspect of opportunity to learn is quantity of schooling – the total amount of time school is open for its statutory purpose, defined by the length of school day and school year. For pupils this time can be reduced by absence or extended by the setting of homework. Evidence gathered since the mid-1970s has consistently shown wide variations in the amount of time schools are open – by as much as 5 hours a week. Similarly, evidence also shows that pupil absence correlates with poorer achievement,[8] and that the provision of homework, even if the demand is relatively small, has a strong impact on achievement.[9]

The time available for schooling is allocated to the different areas of the curriculum, and these decisions, whether taken by schools or individual teachers, determine pupils' curriculum entitlement, and the breadth and balance of the curriculum they experience. Not surprisingly, this aspect of primary practice has attracted considerable attention since the mid-1970s, and the consistency of the findings is remarkable – that on average about half of all curriculum time is allocated to mathematics and language work. What this indicates is that the high-level political and ideological winds that have characterized debate about primary education over the years have hardly ruffled practice on the ground. Primary teachers are not as fickle as they are sometimes assumed to be.

Studies also pointed to considerable variation in curriculum allocation between schools, and between classes in the same school. In a study of the effects of open-plan schools we spent considerable amounts of time observing what pupils actually received as a curriculum, and the extent to which they were involved in it. Figure 9.1 is taken from this study and is based on continuous observation over a whole week in each classroom of

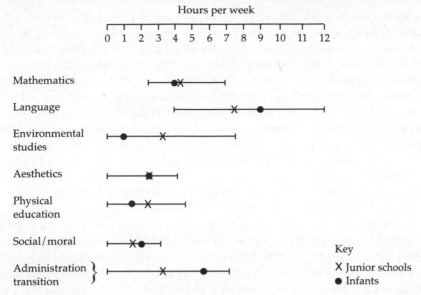

Figure 9.1 Time spent on different curriculum areas

a national sample of infant and junior schools.[10] It shows, for example, that although the average amount of time spent on maths in junior schools was $4^{1}/_{4}$ hours a week, the amount varied from 2 hours a week in some class-rooms to 7 hours a week in others. Similarly, the average amount of time spent on language was $7^{1}/_{2}$ hours a week, but varied from 4 to 12 hours a week. The number of subjects comprising the curriculum varied from five to ten, as did the phasing of time allocations across the days of the week. Some teachers felt that maths, for example, should be taught daily, others were more flexible, while a minority felt that no regular commitment was necessary.

Slightly more time was devoted to maths and language in infant classes, as might be expected, but the most significant difference between infant and junior school time use was that spent on transition activities – that is, time between activities including cleaning up, waiting, moving to a new location, getting dressed after PE, etc. Nearly 6 hours per week were con-sumed by these activities – about 20 per cent of the total available time. More recently Evans *et al.* have also reported on the extent of what they call 'evaporated time' and the implications of its loss to teaching time.[11]

The picture presented in Figure 9.1, although from 1980, is not dissimi-lar to that portrayed 10 years later, after the implementation of the National Curriculum. HMI, in reporting on this, observed that of the 21 hours' teaching time in infant schools, about 70 per cent was devoted to the core subjects.[12] This was made up of approximately 7 hours for English (33 per cent of teaching time), 5 hours for mathematics (23 per cent) and 3 hours for science (14 per cent). There were wide differences in time allocations which were largely explained by the different views held by the schools as to what constituted the subject, and how much time was attributed to it across the curriculum. Variations in English were from 2 hours to 12 hours, in mathematics from 1 hour to 10 hours, and in science from 1 to 8 hours. In a later survey, inspectors expressed concern that few schools had planned the amount of time spent on each subject with any degree of accuracy. Time allocations were generally left to the class teacher and this had led to wide disparities. They also argued that the amount of time devoted to core subjects was not always well used.[13]

Having carried out much of this research in the late 1970s I had a strong sense of *déjà vu* when, in the mid-1990s, as a member of the Dearing review of the National Curriculum, the first thing presented to us was a list of time allocations for each subject to which the review had to conform. The fact is that there is no such thing as *the* primary curriculum, even with a nationally mandated scheme. The balance of curriculum activities achieved in each classroom is unique, as are the patterns of pupil response. There is no suggestion here that a best balance exists, only a need to caution that different curricula are likely to result in different patterns of pupil knowledge acquisition.

Pupil involvement

If we conceive curriculum allocation as the opportunity that is afforded pupils to study a given curriculum area, then pupil involvement is the use that pupils make of that opportunity. It has numerous synonyms in the research literature – attention, time on task, task engagement, to name but a few. However, all are concerned with what pupils actually do with the work they are assigned (or, in some classrooms, are allowed to choose).

The importance of pupil involvement for achievement has been recognized for a long time. William James, for example, wrote in 1899: 'whether the attention comes by grace of genius or by dint of will, the longer one attends to a topic the more mastery of it one has'.[14] In other words, attention, or task involvement, is a necessary condition for learning. Several studies have reported positive relationships between involvement and learning, the latest concluding 'the relationship between time and learning was strong and consistent'.[15]

As with allocation, the research findings on pupil involvement are remarkably consistent. On average pupils are involved in their work 60–66 per cent of their time.[16] However, huge variations are apparent from subject to subject, from class to class and from pupil to pupil in the same classroom. We found in the open-plan school study, for example, that in some classrooms involvement was higher than 80 per cent, while in others it was less than 50 per cent. This range of variation is also true of different subject areas, involvement being lowest in English and maths, those subject areas allocated most time. Similarly, it has consistently been shown that high-achieving children display considerably higher levels of involvement than their low-achieving counterparts.

The opportunity to learn model was, and is, useful in providing a framework within which to discuss time factors in teaching and learning. It has illustrated that the primary curriculum, even after the implementation of the National Curriculum, is what each school, or teacher, decides it is, and that, in addition, large variations exist in the length of school day, the time pupils spend on their work, and how teachers spend and manage their time. The model thus highlights important issues relating to entitlement, balance and breadth. Nevertheless, as a theory of teaching and learning, it has severe limitations. Gaining a child's attention or involvement is a necessary, but by no means sufficient, condition for learning. High levels of pupil involvement are to no avail if curriculum tasks are of poor quality or not related to pupils' capabilities. So, in stressing the quantification of time, the model says nothing about the quality of that time. Thus, in order to achieve a deeper understanding of primary practice, there had to be a shift of direction from quantity to quality.

Task processes

Through the late 1970s and early 1980s there was a developing shift in perceptions of children as learners from behaviourist to constructivist perspectives – that is, from viewing children as passive recipients of knowledge, to active interpreters and constructors of knowledge. From this latter perspective teaching affects achievement through pupil thinking – that is, pupils have to make sense of, or construct, new information in the light of what they already know. And pupil thinking and teaching are mediated by the curriculum tasks and activities that teachers provide. Thus to understand the impact of teaching on learning requires the identification of the quality of such tasks in terms of the extent to which their demands are appropriate to, or match, pupils' capabilities. Further, since pupil thinking takes place within a complex social context, it is also necessary to understand the impact of social processes on children's task performances.

This analysis underpinned our 1984 study which focused on classroom task processes through the concept of match, or appropriateness.[17] The model which we developed is shown in Figure 9.2. Briefly, the assumptions underpinning the model are that teaching is a purposeful activity, and that teacher purposes or intentions inform their selection or design of tasks. The tasks are presented or specified in some manner, within a

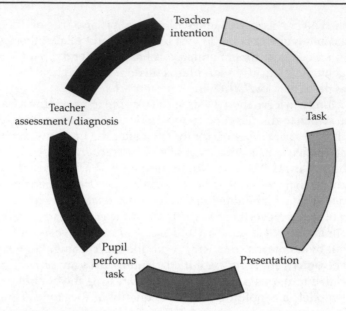

Figure 9.2 A model of classroom task processes

system of classroom organization and management set up by the teacher. The pupils then work on their tasks, demonstrating through their performances their understandings of them. When the work is completed it might be expected that the teacher will assess it, feeding that assessment back to the learners, as well as forward to inform their next intentions. The process is thus cyclic. This description is deceptively simple, however, because of the possibility of a mismatch or an inappropriate link between every pair of elements in the model.

We therefore gathered data on teacher intentions, the tasks themselves, the manner of their presentation or specification, pupils' work on the tasks and their understandings or misconceptions of them, and teacher assessments or diagnosis of these understandings, in order to characterize the intellectual demands of the tasks and the extent to which they were matched. From these data it was apparent that the tasks teachers set do not always embody their intentions; for example over one-fifth of all tasks observed failed to meet their intended aim. The actual intellectual demand apparent in the majority of tasks in language and mathematics was limited to increments in knowledge or skill, and practice. There was little opportunity for the application of knowledge in new contexts or for the active discovery of new knowledge and skills. Approximately 40 per cent of tasks matched pupils' capabilities, but there was a strong trend towards the underestimation of higher-attaining children and a corresponding overestimation of low-attaining pupils. Teachers tended to stress the procedural aspects of tasks and mechanical progress through a scheme of work, rather than pupil understanding.

These analyses of the interactions of pupils and tasks were supplemented by data on the nature and content of exchanges between teachers and pupils during the assessment and diagnosis of completed work. These show that teachers were not highly skilled in diagnosis. Rarely did they identify the sources of pupils' misunderstandings or misconceptions, and the typical crisis management style adopted exacerbated these problems.

These findings were similar to those reported by HMI, and were drawn upon in a report by the House of Commons Select Committee which concluded that 'the skills of diagnosing learning success and difficulty, and selecting and presenting new tasks are the essence of the teacher's profession and vital to children's progress'.[18]

We were also conscious in this study that another factor mediating the quality of pupil thinking and task completion was the social context in which pupils work. In most primary schools the immediate social context of learning is the classroom group of some four to six children, although the composition of these groups, in terms of ability, sex, age, etc. varies from class to class, and sometimes from subject to subject. The Plowden Report, although prescribing the individualization of learning, claimed many advantages for group work,[19] but few of these have been supported empirically. The evidence indicates a certain ambivalence, or confusion, among teachers, in that they tend to sit children in groups but prefer to retain individualized tasks rather than introduce cooperative work. In other words children sit *in* groups but do not work *as* groups. The unfortunate outcome of this is a high level of low-quality talk and a dearth of cooperative endeavour.[20] A major component of our work since the mid-1980s has thus been the improvement of children's task experiences through the design and implementation of genuine cooperative group work.[21] Interestingly, in the light of the opportunity to learn model, we have been able to show improvements in terms of both increases in pupil task involvement and in better quality of social interaction.

The model of task processes shown in Figure 9.2 has proved to be extremely useful for addressing several policy-related issues centring on the quality or appropriateness of pupil experiences. Our study in the late 1980s of the education of 4-year-olds in school utilized this same model,[22] as did our follow-through study of children transferring from special to ordinary schools as a consequence of the move to mainstreaming.[23]

Nevertheless, valuable as it is, the model has its drawbacks. It allows the identification of typical weaknesses among primary teachers in matching, in the diagnosis of children's understandings, and in linking their intentions and tasks, but does not contain factors sufficient to explain these. Yet without adequate explanation there can be no effective attempts at improving practice.

Teacher knowledge

In contemplating what these factors might be, we reasoned that for teachers effectively to diagnose children's understandings, to plan appropriate tasks, to present quality explanations and demonstrations, and to make curricular choices, knowledge and understanding of subject matter are required. This, in turn, raises such important concerns as how teachers can teach well knowledge that they do not fully understand, make clear decisions about development or progression in curriculum areas with which they are not thoroughly conversant, and accurately diagnose children's understandings and misconceptions without an adequate knowledge of the subject.

Questions of this kind are not of course new. John Dewey argued in the 1930s that to recognize opportunities for early mathematical learning one must know mathematics, to recognize opportunities for elementary scientific learning one must know physics, chemistry, biology and geology, and so on down the list of fields of knowledge. More recently, the Department of Education and Science asserted that 'the greatest obstacle to the continued improvement of science in primary schools is that many existing teachers lack a working knowledge of elementary science',[24] and this has been supported in a set of studies on primary school teachers' understandings of science concepts.[25] These reported that the majority of teachers' views were based on a 'mixture of intuitive beliefs and half remembered text book science from their school days, sometimes with incorrect or imprecise use of scientific language', and concluded that the scientific thinking of many of the teachers studied resembled that of children.

Our own national surveys have revealed that teachers feel insecure with their subject knowledge in several areas of the curriculum.[26] In only English and maths did more than half say they felt confident with their existing knowledge. In both surveys less than 35 per cent of teachers felt competent to teach science, music or technology without substantial in-service support. In technology only 14 per cent perceived themselves as competent. Indeed, when questioned about their competences within subject areas, they claimed particular difficulties with things electronic or related to information technology.

In the United States Shulman warned of the neglect of teachers' knowledge in research on teaching, and identified seven types of knowledge teachers require for effective teaching.[27] On the basis of these he developed a cyclic model of pedagogical reasoning and action which shares many similarities with our own model of task processes. This model is shown in Figure 9.3. Briefly, the model assumes that teachers must first comprehend the ideas to be taught and the purposes to be achieved. They must then transform their knowledge and understandings into tasks which are both

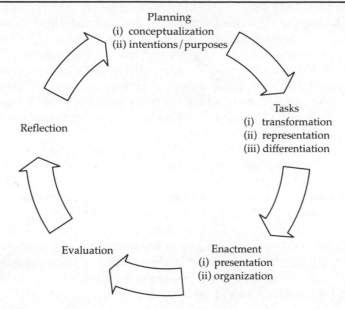

Figure 9.3 A model of pedagogical reasoning

suitable for the age group taught, and appropriately differentiated to cater for the range of achievement in the class. This transformation should also consider how the central ideas can best be represented – in terms of analogues, metaphors, examples, etc. Teaching then takes place within a classroom organization and management structure set up by the teacher. Assessment or evaluation of pupils' understanding follows, along with reflection by the teacher on the success or otherwise of the lesson, and its form and content. This in turn leads back to comprehension, and a new beginning.

This appeared to be a fruitful model to guide research into the role of teacher knowledge in teaching performance, an area which, by the early 1990s, had attained a high priority not only because of the implementation of the National Curriculum, with its demand for specified content, but also because of doubts, at governmental level at least, about the quality of teacher training. HMI inspections of primary teacher training courses were, by then, showing concern about time allocations to subjects.[28] In science, for example, HMI claimed that courses were too short to ensure student teachers' understanding of the progressive development of children's scientific thinking, or to develop a knowledge base on which to work with confidence. It similarly complained about time devoted to the humanities, leading to a generally poor knowledge base, and inadequate matching of work to children's levels of understanding, and assessment of pupil learning. The advice of the National Curriculum Council on teacher training also set out clear prescriptions for the extent of subject knowledge in the core and foundation subjects.[29]

So what knowledge do primary student teachers have on entry to, and exit from, PGCE training courses? And what is the relationship between student teachers' knowledge and their teaching performance? These were the core questions in a study which we subsequently published under the title *Learning to Teach*,[30] using a modified version of the model presented in Figure 9.3.

Assessments of the knowledge necessary to teach to level 6 in the core subjects of the National Curriculum were administered to cohorts of PGCE students in the first and last weeks of their courses, together with wider measures of beliefs and attitudes to teaching and to subjects. The findings showed that in science and mathematics these graduates showed only a basic understanding of many of the topics they are obliged to teach in the National Curriculum, and as in the Summers and Kruger studies, the misconceptions they displayed in these subjects were similar to those found in primary pupils.[31] More generally, their knowledge of the structure of the disciplines, even of that which they had recently graduated in, was poor.

With regard to the link between knowledge and teaching performance, the groups with high levels of appropriate knowledge taught at consistently higher levels of competence than other students, in both the planning and interactive stages of teaching. The impact of the lack of, or partial, knowledge showed itself in their inability to develop or extend a theme, or failure to model a lesson. These findings cannot be used to argue that subject knowledge is the be-all and end-all of successful teaching; it is a necessary, but not sufficient, ingredient.

Alexander *et al.* accepted that training courses are overcrowded, but averred that beginning teachers do require specialist subject knowledge.[32] Thus one of the implications of our findings concerned the extent to which such knowledge could be developed and extended in a one-year PGCE course. Unfortunately political events were running far faster than the research evidence could be gathered or assimilated. The then Secretary of State ruled that such knowledge could best be acquired by the apprenticeship of student teachers to those very teachers who, on their own admission, do not possess that knowledge!

Another way to manage this dilemma is to assume teacher learning as a continuous process and search for ways of facilitating that development. Alexander *et al.* argued that it would be unreasonable to suppose that initial training could prepare all teachers for all aspects of their professional work and for schools to expect that they will receive fully fledged practitioners. They thus argued that initial training should be a preparation for the early years of teaching and a foundation on which subsequent training and development can build. To make this effective, however, there has to be a clearly understood division of labour between the initial, induction and in-service stages of training.

This proposal, although dripping with common sense, begs many questions regarding optimum strategies for professional development. Teachers' professional development is inadequately theorized and researched, and there is a lack of clarity about the type of theoretical framework necessary to guide professional development and course design.[33] What research exists suggests that sustained changes or improvements in practice will occur only if teachers' theories, knowledge and belief systems can be influenced. For example, Brown and MacIntyre argue that any serious attempts to innovate in classrooms have to start from where teachers are and how they construe their own teaching, their pupils and what they are trying to do.[34] As such priority needs to be given to how best to understand more about teachers' knowledge, their conceptual frameworks, how they vary and how they relate to the structural, organizational and cultural contexts in which they work.

Teacher theories

This is, in fact, a broader spin on the relationship of teacher knowledge and teaching performance, and is represented in the research literature under the label 'teacher theories and action'. The purpose of this field, in general terms, is to make explicit the frames of reference through which teachers perceive and progress information on the assumption that teachers' cognitive and pedagogical behaviours are guided by, and make sense in relation to, a personally held system of beliefs, values and principles. What is needed from this perspective, therefore, are clear explications of teachers' knowledge and beliefs and their relationship to practice so that programmes of professional development can enhance practice through the development of teacher thinking.

This is an area in which we are currently working with reception teachers, focusing on the role of play in young children's learning. Here is yet another area where there is a gulf between rhetoric and reality. Early childhood educators argue that play is the bedrock of young children's learning, but observations of play show that play activities tend to be of poor quality. In this study we are therefore combining our desire to improve aspects of practice with the development of better theory. In pursuit of this we have developed a model of the relationships between teacher theories and practice (Figure 9.4). This draws on our definition of teachers' knowledge as their personal stock of information, skills, experiences, beliefs and memories, and assumes that sets of knowledge of different aspects of their work combine to become a theory or ideology. These theories can be narrow or broad. For example, a teacher's theory of play

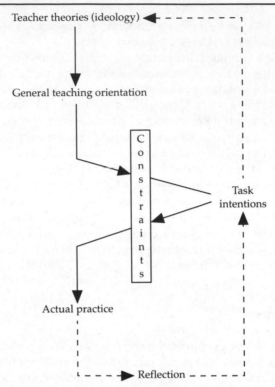

Figure 9.4 Hypothesized relationship of teachers' theories and classroom practice

will draw on, and be built upon, a particular set of understandings and beliefs, but this theory of play will in turn be but one element of his or her broader theory of teaching in the early years. These theories are instrumental in teachers' conceptions and constructions of what they believe to be appropriate learning environments, and this is shown in Figure 9.4 as their general teaching orientation. The extent to which teachers are able to fulfil their ideal teaching orientations through the activities they plan for their pupils will depend on sets of mediating factors or constraints. The constraints which operate between teaching orientation and teachers' task intentions could include factors at classroom, school, local or national level, such as classroom space, the availability of resources and equipment, the number and characteristics of children, school policy on class size and teaching assistance, perceptions of parental priorities, and the demands of the National Curriculum. Similarly, whether teachers' intentions are realized in practice will rest on another, but overlapping, set of factors including the reaction of children to the activity, the amount of adult help, and the time and resources available. Finally, whether, or how, practice changes, and the effect of changes on teachers' theories, will depend on the extent to which teachers are able, enabled, or willing to reflect on links between intentions and practice, and from these to their underpinning theories. Data have thus been gathered from teachers' accounts, interviews and stimulated recall techniques to cast light on each of the elements in this model as a first step to gaining enhanced understandings of effective professional development approaches.[35]

Conclusion

Our individual voyages have been well recorded over the years, but each record has provided only a limited, if distinctive, view of how the primary terrain has been mapped from one particular perspective. Lacking have been considerations of the interlinked purposes and motives behind these forays, insights into the choices and designs of the routes taken, and details of the cumulative body of knowledge and understandings acquired. The explication of these has been the prime aim of this paper.

The common thread through this story is the constant search for, and development of, better models and theories to enhance our understanding of primary practice. And intertwined with this has been a more general paradigm shift from behaviourists to constructivist perspectives, which not only challenged accepted beliefs about the role of pupils in their own learning, but also redirected research attention away from a focus on teachers' classroom behaviours, to aspects of teacher knowledge and thought.

These theories have been differentially useful. The teaching styles approach, in attempting to thrust all teachers into one of two boxes variously labelled traditional–progressive, formal–informal, etc. was, in retrospect, doomed to failure if the purpose was better to conceptualize primary practice, and thus had to be abandoned. The opportunity to learn model was more useful in this respect, allowing a quantitative framework of time allocations and use at the level of school, curriculum, task and pupil. But time is an empty box which needs filling with worthwhile content, and attention thus necessarily shifted to models which focused on the nature and quality of classroom tasks, and teachers' abilities to develop and manage these effectively. This focus highlighted the importance of teacher knowledge of subject matter, curriculum and pedagogy, and raised, along the way, crucial questions about the nature, quantity and timing of teacher training at pre- and in-service levels. The most recent theoretical shift, to concentrate on teachers' broader theories, knowledge and beliefs, reflects these concerns by containing the assumption that these theories, which are often implicit, bear directly on the type and quality of teachers' classroom actions. In other words, the quality of classroom practice can be improved by enhancing the quality of teachers' thinking, which, in turn, has begun to spotlight the crucial importance of the planning or preactive stage of teaching.

Finally, what the cumulative data from these multiple perspectives clearly demonstrate is the tremendous complexity of primary practice, and in consequence the high levels of skill and knowledge required by practitioners. These include, as a minimum: to be thoroughly conversant with various bodies of knowledge; to be skilled in task design, and in the differentiation of tasks to cater for pupils of differing capabilities; to be knowledgeable about alternative modes of task presentation, in relation to individual, group and whole-class work; to be skilled in the assessment and diagnosis of pupils' understandings and misconceptions; to organize classroom settings which are both fit for particular task purposes, and to maintain high levels of pupil involvement; to be able to monitor effectively a variety of classroom events and act accordingly; to generate and maintain pupil interest and enthusiasm; to create and maintain good social relationships; to relate well to and work with parents and other outside agencies. This list could be much more extensive, but the purpose here is not to be all-embracing. Rather it is to set an agenda around which those of us interested in the continued improvement of primary practice can rally and focus our efforts. The current fragmentation of professional support for teachers must make this our future priority.

Notes

1 S.N. Bennett, 'The effective primary school teacher: the search for a theory of pedagogy', *Teaching and Teacher Education*, 4, 19–30 (1988).
2 Central Advisory Council for Education (CACE), *Children and Their Primary Schools* (London: HMSO, 1967).
3 Department of Education and Science, *Primary Education in England: A Survey by HM Inspectors of Schools* (London: HMSO, 1978).
4 M. Galton, B. Simon and P. Croll, *Inside the Primary Classroom* (London: Routledge & Kegan Paul, 1980).
5 R.M. Giaconia and L.V. Hedges, 'Identifying features of effective open education', *Review of Educational Research*, 52, 579–612 (1983); J. Gray and D. Satterly, 'Formal or informal? A reassessment of the British evidence', *British Journal of Educational Psychology*, 51, 187–96 (1982); W.S. Anthony, 'Research on progressive teaching', *British Journal of Educational Psychology*, 52, 381–5 (1982).
6 S.N. Bennett, 'Educational research and the media', *Westminster Studies in Education*, 1, 23–30 (1978).
7 J.B. Carroll, 'A model of school learning', *Teachers College Record*, 64, 723–33 (1963); B.S. Bloom, *Human Characteristics and School Learning* (New York: McGraw-Hill, 1976); A. Harnischfeger and D.E. Wiley, *Teaching–Learning Processes in the Elementary School: A Synoptic View*, Studies of Education Processes No. 9 (Chicago: University of Chicago, 1975).

8 K. Fogelman, 'School attendance, attainment and behaviour', *British Journal of Educational Psychology*, 48, 148–58 (1978).

9 A. Alton-Lee and G. Nuthall, 'Pupil experiences and pupil learning in the elementary classroom: an illustration of a generative methodology', *Teaching and Teacher Education*, 6, 27–46 (1990).

10 S.N. Bennett, J. Andreae, P. Hegarty and B. Wade, *Open Plan Schools: Teaching, Curriculum, Design* (Slough: National Foundation for Educational Research, 1980).

11 L. Evans, A. Pickwood, S.R.St J. Neills and R.J. Campbell, *The Meaning of Infant Teachers' Work* (London: Routledge, 1994).

12 Department of Education and Science, *The Implications of the National Curriculum in Primary Schools* (London: HMSO, 1989).

13 Office for Standards in Education, *The Teaching and Learning of Number in Primary Schools* (London: HMSO, 1993).

14 W. James, *The Principles of Psychology* (London: Routledge & Kegan Paul, 1899).

15 Alton-Lee and Nuthall, 'Pupil experiences and pupil learning in the elementary classroom'.

16 D. Boydell, 'Pupil behaviour in junior classrooms', *British Journal of Educational Psychology*, 45, 122–9 (1975); A. Pollard, P. Broadfoot, P. Croll, M. Osborne and D. Abbott, *Changing English Primary Schools* (London: Cassell, 1994); Bennett *et al.*, *Open Plan Schools*; Galton *et al.*, *Inside the Primary Classroom*; R.J. Alexander, *Policy and Practice in Primary Education* (London: Routledge, 1992).

17 S.N. Bennett, C. Desforges, A. Cockburn and B. Wilkinson, *The Quality of Pupil Learning Experiences* (Hove: Lawrence Erlbaum, 1984).

18 House of Commons Education, Science and Arts Committee, *Achievement in Primary Schools* (London: HMSO, 1986).

19 CACE, *Children and Their Primary Schools*.

20 Galton *et al.*, *Inside the Primary Classroom*; Bennett *et al.*, *The Quality of Pupil Learning Experiences*.

21 S.N. Bennett and A. Cass, 'The effects of group composition on group interactive processes and pupil understanding', *British Education Research Journal*, 15, 19–32 (1988); S.N. Bennett and E. Dunne, *Managing Classroom Groups* (London: Simon and Schuster, 1992).

22 S.N. Bennett and J. Kell, *A Good Start? Four Year Olds in Infant Schools* (Oxford: Blackwell, 1989).

23 S.N. Bennett and A. Cass, *From Special to Ordinary Schools: Case Studies in Integration* (London: Cassell, 1989).

24 Department of Education and Science, *Better Schools* (London: HMSO, 1985).

25 M. Summers and C. Kruger, 'A longitudinal study of a constructivist approach to improving primary school teachers' subject matter knowledge in science', *Teaching and Teacher Education*, 10, 499–520 (1994); C. Kruger and M. Summers, 'An investigation of some primary teachers' understandings of changes in materials', *School Science Review*, 71, 17–27 (1989).

26 E. Wragg, S.N. Bennett and C. Carre, 'Primary teachers and the National Curriculum', *Research Papers in Education*, 4, 17–37 (1989); S.N. Bennett, E. Wragg, C. Carre and D. Carter, 'A longitudinal study of primary teachers' perceived competence in, and concerns about National Curriculum implementation', *Research Papers in Education*, 7, 53–78 (1992).

27 L.S. Shulman, 'Those who understand: knowledge growth in teaching', *Educational Researcher*, 15, 4–14 (1986); L.S. Shulman, 'Knowledge and teaching: foundations of the new reforms', *Harvard Educational Review*, 57, 1–22 (1987).

28 Department of Education and Science, *The Professional Training of Primary School Teachers* (London: HMSO, 1991).

29 National Curriculum Council, *The National Curriculum and the Initial Training of Students, Articled and Licensed Teachers* (York: National Curriculum Council, 1991).

30 S.N. Bennett and C. Carré, *Learning to Teach* (London: Routledge, 1993).

31 Summers and Kruger, 'A longitudinal study of a constructivist approach'.

32 R.J. Alexander, J. Rose and C. Woodhead, *Curriculum Organisation and Classroom Practice in Primary Schools* (London: HMSO, 1992).

33 W. Doyle, 'Themes in teacher education research' in W.R. Houston (ed.), *Handbook of Research on Teacher Education* (New York: MacMillan, 1990); C. Day, 'The importance of learning biography in supporting teacher development: an empirical study', in C. Day, J. Calderhead and P. Denicolo (eds), *Research on Teacher Thinking: Understanding Personal Development* (London: Falmer, 1993).

34 S. Brown and D. MacIntyre, *Making Sense of Teaching* (Buckingham: Open University Press, 1993).

35 S.N. Bennett, L. Wood and S. Rogers, *Teaching Through Play: Teachers' Thinking and Classroom Practice* (Buckingham: Open University Press, 1995).

10

A vision: the twenty-first-century primary school

David Winkley

Midsomer Primary School does not look very different from the schools we saw in the late 1990s, when one or two schools won design awards for combining sensitivity to the local environment with flexibility of use – there is extensive use of screening, for instance, to make different combinations of spaces, from small and quiet to large and open. Midsomer has excellent resource bases, with easy access to a variety of computer facilities. There are video projection facilities in the main hall, which doubles as a drama centre. Health and library centres are attached to the school and next door is a senior citizen drop-in and residential centre. Childstart (the mother and parent support organization linked to social services) has an office in the school next to the health workers' office (paid for out of the GP budget). There is a small library for parents and a strong and healthy tradition of volunteer parents and workers in the school itself. A supportive governing body draws the interests of the school and the community together. Outside there are exploratory play facilities with an artificial grass and floodlit multi-base games centre. Around these is a carefully controlled 'wild pond' for pond dipping and plant study. We are particularly pleased with the use of the work of young local artists and sculptors, which has been carefully and imaginatively placed around the site.

Staffing

There are some striking differences these days in the way the school is staffed. We have long come to realize that it is the quality of teacher–pupil

interaction in the classroom that makes the difference to the learning outcome. Teachers come from all walks of life, are highly trained graduates
and are to be distinguished from tutors who only teach those aspects of the
curriculum in which they have specialized knowledge. Teachers have the
overall responsibility for supervising the learning progress of their pupils.
They take an overview, manage the programme of study, assess and lead
the team of support personnel. They create a learning culture in the school,
create a sense of community and have advanced qualifications in the practice of teaching. They are assessed vigorously by their peers in their largely
practical, class-based training period and there are various levels which
they can attain through postgraduate, school-based training. Heads of
schools are always 'master teachers' who have additional training in
management.

The four key management themes of the moment are:

- Time management: ensuring that the greatest possible impact is made
  on the pupils through every activity.
- Standards control: ensuring that pupils' learning experiences, in and
  out of school, are of the highest quality.
- Leadership of people: learning to motivate staff and children and create
  an extremely positive culture. Special attention is now paid to leadership skills in the appointing, training and supporting of head teachers.
- Management of resources: we now know more about how best to determine and deploy resources to achieve identifiable results. All schools
  now have trained bursars who manage budgets under the direction of
  heads, governors and staff.

Because of the changing and much more open nature of schooling,
teachers have more involvement with other professionals, including business colleagues and people with specialist expertise in various non-
educational fields. Teachers also have extensive experience in student
support and mentoring, as many more students are in schools these days.
Teachers in primary schools still take on a generalist brief, with responsibility for an overview of children's learning, but tutors and other teachers
may often take on some specialist teaching functions. However, every
teacher is able to teach at least one subject, or subject area, in considerable
depth.

As a consequence of all this, teaching is a more prestigious profession
than it used to be and is better paid. Teachers manage their own profession
through the General Teaching Council and there is a highly effective information support service which now networks the whole of the UK. Quality
work, major teaching initiatives, local publications and curriculum programmes of high quality are now disseminated or purchased through networks. Teaching has become a profession very much in demand.

Specialist skills

There have, in recent years, been striking changes in the way teaching is managed. In addition to the 'core' teaching staff, a variety of consultant teaching staff is used on a part-time basis to deliver some of the very precisely planned curriculum programmes. The use of practising artists, musicians, dancers, technicians and engineers is particularly notable, and improved achievement in these practical areas has been observed.

Consultant staff (or tutors) are usually specialist teachers who work at developing the abilities of all their pupils, but also engage in advanced work with particularly interested and talented children. This has had a particular impact on the motivation and skills of inner-city children. It is to our credit, for example, that every child in the UK now learns a musical instrument, beginning with a minimum course of basic lessons, and leading – if the child shows talent – to advanced levels of achievement. Parents are encouraged these days to have specialist training to help them support schools more effectively. Some part-time posts are available for parents with a minimum training qualification. These are local parents who may be trained to help delivery of particular aspects of curriculum programmes or perhaps attached to a particular child because he/she has a learning need of one kind or another. In addition, all schools have a full- or part-time technician, a school librarian and a child counsellor who also works with parents, which brings them up to the standard of primary schools in Washington State, USA, in 1994.

Many more students are also seen in schools these days working both with the pre-planned curriculum programmes and under the supervision of the class teachers, some of whom will have a specialist interest in mentoring. There is a variety of types of student – students of teaching, of tutoring, of parent helpers and classroom assistants. Only the student teacher is required to be a graduate, but there is a legal requirement of a minimum of one teacher per 30 children. This number seems high and has not fallen over the years (in fact it has risen slightly), but this needs to be set against the evidence of additional, trained adults working with each class and the increased use these days of specialist group work often supervised by tutors, consultants or other support personnel such as classroom assistants, or trained parents.

Curriculum

The curriculum in primary schools is strikingly different, though looking back we can see the beginnings of change in the early 1990s. The National Curriculum of the 1988 Act has been slimmed down dramatically and rather resembles in presentation the Scottish version of the 1990s. (The higher achievements of Scottish children throughout the 1980s and 1990s helped support the anti-1988 Act movement in England and Wales, though more recent research evidence suggests it was attributable, probably, to greater school stability and higher teacher morale.)

Targets

The curriculum of the twenty-first century has three main strands. The first is a very strong focus on key targets in achievement for the early years. This is managed through very early continuous assessment of milestones carried out by paediatricians, health workers, nursery nurses and teachers. Children appearing to fail against the base-line academic milestones have intensive support from ages 4 to 7 to ensure that 98 per cent of children have reached the baseline targets at age 7 in basic reading and arithmetical skills. (It has taken western Europe more than 25 years to catch up, here, with Japanese standards in the late 1980s.) This support is carefully tailor-made to individual children. We have learned now how very different children's intellectual and emotional approaches to learning are, and we understand more about how to match a teaching process to a learning need. Much more use is made of individualized computer programs, parent training and support, and confidence building. During the last decade there has been a widely expanded use of sophisticated information technology. New programmes access a vast range of information, helping individual learners develop skills and interests, and tackle specific learning blocks. Computer programs now supplement work in all curriculum areas and networking allows pupils and teachers to communicate beyond the boundaries of the school – into other schools, and even into the home.

However, personal relationships still remain central to successful teaching.

There is a strong and systematic emphasis on positive reward, and teachers these days are highly trained in interactive skills. Teachers in the early years have high social esteem these days (only last year two infant teachers, rated master teachers, were appointed to the Second Chamber, and the new, classless equivalent of the old MBE is a common sign of national recognition). There was, by 2001, a firm understanding, substantially based on research evidence, that highly specialized, high-quality teaching in the early years made a significant difference in the long run to the social and emotional outcome of pupils. The LEA experiments of 1994, putting substantial extra resources into the early years, meant that by 2015 a remarkably high proportion of pupils from inner-city backgrounds went on to higher education. There was in the 2010–15 period an equally striking fall in juvenile crime.

Planned components

Secondly, the curriculum is now shaped into a myriad of planned components. The objective of curricular programmes in Stages 1 and 2 is very much to provide children with the best possible facility to develop all their talents and interests as rapidly and as far as possible on their learning journey. There are sets of minimum base-line objectives in maths, science, language and the arts but these are expressed in and extended by subject specialist programmes of study. Children are, from the age of 9 onwards, also encouraged to opt into programmes that particularly match their interests and abilities.

For example, all children are expected to take a specified number of music programmes with a view to reaching the base-lines in instrument playing, knowledge of musical cultures and basic composition, but those children who emerge through the assessments as showing particular talents in music would be given extra time to work at more advanced levels. All schools now have specialist teachers to teach these advanced levels, as well as many of the base-line levels. Many are brought in on a consultancy basis to teach part-time on particular programmes.

There are new key emphases in the curriculum. One development has been the compulsory component in the curriculum on parenting at Stage 2 (ages 7–11), partly taught by highly specialist staff attached to the school. Generally, more emphasis is placed on teaching health and parenting – the skills necessary to have a fulfilled home life – at quite a young age. There are new programmes focusing on democracy and the meaning and significance of citizenship: these programmes are linked by external references to economics and politics, and by self-reference to a philosophy of personal behaviour and responsibility in a twenty-first-century democracy. Tolerance for others, the role of minorities and issues of equal opportunities are examined in some depth.

All children begin in Stage 2 (and continue in greater depth in Stages 3 and 4) to study the world of work and leisure. Children now have more understanding of the richness and variety of work and leisure opportunities, of how careers can be flexible, of common components, such as problem-solving and teamworking, and the rewards of imaginative activity and fulfilling achievements for the individual who is prepared to keep thinking, practising and learning.

Moral education now has a number of dimensions: it is understood that our sense of values derives substantially from our inheritance, and culture, and in particular from our early experiences of relationships at home, in the community and at school. Moral values are studied in various programmes (including those on home life, religion and citizenship) but are also addressed through a continuous concern with the individual's self-understanding. Children are systematically encouraged, not only to understand what the valuing of others *means*, but also to reflect on their own strengths and weaknesses and on the meaning of insight. It is recognized that this can only be achieved in a home and school culture that is itself calm, kind, considerate, firm, balanced and good-humoured.

These days the programmes are themselves planned very carefully by experienced teachers. Such teachers are identified by the National Information System as a consequence of much improved in-service training which focuses on practical skills in the classroom. The key qualification here is the Master of Teaching Studies degree (MTS) awarded on the basis of closely assessed classroom and in-school performance. It is, for the most part, holders of the MTS who are responsible for the teams of teachers who develop the curriculum programmes. These are very detailed and imaginative descriptions of actual teaching and learning events in classrooms 'shaped', like narratives, to make as much sense as possible to children. They are closely evaluated by teachers and children and are constantly updated, modified or replaced. Already these are forming large curricular banks of practical, highly developed and imaginative components – planned series of lessons – which can be interconnected in various subject combinations.

Some programmes are being used in many countries, and all are being evaluated constantly and reassessed by the teachers. National curricula are still in place in some countries, but the compulsory components have been thinned down everywhere. Finland and Denmark led the way by abandoning the notion of a national curriculum in the 1990s. The UK National Curriculum is a slimmed down version of the Scottish NC developed in the late 1980s, and is now no more than an outline syllabus, frequently reassessed. Day-to-day classroom practice focuses largely on the planned programmes. It is worth adding here that there is far better continuity between primary and secondary sectors, with precision in matching programmes of study to individuals. Considerable thought has gone into ensuring as smooth and effective transition as possible. Schools and curriculum programmes are less driven by bureaucratic, institutional or timetabling demands, and are more able to respond to the needs of individuals. Teachers are very careful to make sure children do not waste time on undemanding or repeated tasks (unlike the 1990s where, on average, 40 per cent of time was spent on routine repetition).

Learning out of school

The third strand of development has, in many respects, been the most striking of all. There has been clear recognition that children spend more than 80 per cent of their waking hours *out* of school. The Children's University and Education Extra are organizations that, typically, encourage learning outside school hours, giving children of different ages information and support to enhance their learning on a wider platform. Schools are also open in the evenings and weekends as community resources, with a wide variety of courses and activities on offer. Children are encouraged to take 'learning paths' so that each experience or assignment builds systematically on another. Schools also spend more planned time liaising with parents and there are many courses available for parents to enable them to gain skills and insight into their own – as well as their children's – learning process.

In general, teachers from the 1990s would, if they saw us now, be struck by three things about the twenty-first-century curriculum: the high standards which children attain; the opportunities and diversity the practical teaching programmes offer; the quality, variety and relevance of the classroom and extra-classroom experiences on offer and their close matching to children's needs. Young children in some schools are taking courses in Latin, modern languages, local history and culture, film and dance as extra core components, often after school or at weekends. Some schools are even developing philosophy as a core subject.

The teaching and learning process

Next, there is the question of the teaching process itself. The very extensive work carried out in the 1970s and 1980s on teaching methods has proved something of a blind alley. This was, surprisingly, predicted by the International Association for the Evaluation of Educational Achievement in 1989 in its extensive study of international classroom practice when it came to the conclusion that effective teaching was dependent on the activities of the student much more than on those of the teacher. Since then we have put far more thought into the best ways of helping individual children learn actively, efficiently and enthusiastically, bearing in mind their own idiosyncratic learning patterns.

We now look very closely at the learning characteristics of learners. An improved version of the old Myers–Briggs personality indicator has been developed into a refined tool offering insights to help the learner understand and develop his character and learning capabilities with the support of the teacher.

Children are thus helped to understand the ways they habitually learn and we are now more technically precise in trying to create an appropriate range of classroom teaching experiences for learning diversity. The key emphasis now is on children understanding themselves, building on strengths and working at compensating for weaknesses (for example, helping to create orderly thinking processes for the naturally chaotic, extending the visual imagination of abstract thinkers, developing social self-confidence in the inhibited). The focus is on developing the individual's ability to learn through a variety of learning styles, some of which may not come naturally.

We aim to encourage children to become self-aware in the way they work and learn: this leads to a concern to improve such critical factors as powers of memory, concentration, reasoning skills, emotional and personal sensitivity, self-awareness, problem-solving and mental play, divergent thinking and imagination. All these are developed through a range of intellectually demanding tasks, from the mathematical and the musical to the linguistic, practical and physical activity – working *independently and self-critically* as well as *with and through others* in cooperative ventures. Children are always encouraged to make learning decisions for themselves; to appreciate their own differences; and to respect the differences of others. Children are encouraged to accept the challenge of living in a multi-cultural society. Personal balance and the development of insight into personal behaviour have thus become a very important aspect of twenty-first-century schooling, and a great deal of thought now goes into ensuring children's emotional and intellectual stability.

The management of behaviour is now seen to be a highly skilled process involving teachers, parents and, sometimes, other professionals in consistently supporting the child. Sanctions and rewards are carefully tailor-made to support the needs and temperaments of individuals and to help children understand the creative potential of being disciplined members of a group and a community. Children sometimes join with staff in monitoring behaviour, identifying and counselling children with problems and taking on some of the responsibilities for the smooth running of the school, though we are careful not to make unreasonable demands: children need space and freedom to grow up, safely protected by supporting adults.

Assessment

Assessments of all kinds are a key component of schooling. All subjects are assessed continuously and there is a dynamic relationship between assessment and the teaching process. Curiously, less time is spent, by and large, than was taken by the enforced examination and assessment system in the 1990s, though the idea of levels has been retained. Teaching programmes are locked into the levels and children are aware what levels they are on. There is now a bench-mark level for all subjects (the base-line) after which children are encouraged to go as far as they can. A modified version of Microsoft's Education Excel is used by many schools to send parents regular information about their children's progress. Extensive feedback of an encouraging kind is also given to all pupils. The old 1990s Standard Assessment Tasks (SATs) have been abandoned, but the best of the SAT material has been retained, improved and linked to curriculum programmes. Assessment is semi-standardized and all children are required to take base-line assessments. These bench-mark levels are certificates of competence which all children are expected to attain, after which they act as passports for future progress.

Children can, if they want, get level awards in any subject area after achieving a base-line (like a 1990s grade exam in music). These higher-level awards are voluntary but many children take them. Publication of results has been abandoned, and all assessments now record not only attainment but also the child's particular skills and strategies in approaching a subject. Levels have been retained but teachers are required to amplify any report by reference to the quality of the pupil's course work and general approach to learning. (Universities, of course, have long abandoned degree grades based on exams, and a student now emerges from one of the great variety of institutions with a detailed report based on close analysis of course work, skills, dedication and learning style.) Standards seem to be very much higher than they used to be, and as a result of the much more varied and motivating teaching arrange-ments virtually all children eventually graduate. This has had an impact on business; for example, 90 per cent of senior managers in the UK are now graduates, compared with 20 per cent in 1993, bringing us level with our competitors.

Overall, our rigorous, continual assessment systems have shown that base-line standards have improved greatly but also each child in its chosen advanced subject choices is far further on from the child of the 1990s. Some children advance on many subject fronts, and some pursue two or more subjects in depth, moving way beyond base-line in language, science and maths. But the real change is that all children advance on at least one front, as well as receiving a wide-ranging exposure to all arts and science sub-jects, up to age 18. This has had an astonishing effect on attitudes towards lifetime enterprise. Basic skills are strong, but there is now an ambition for all children to develop practical skills, wisdom and maturity to the limit of their talent and ambition.

Research and school improvement

The role of empirical research is now better understood. We have a deep-ening understanding of the relationship between theory and practice, and of how to take into account the practical implications of new ideas. (We now have a clearer idea of how principles are influenced by belief, how principles influence practices, and what it means in a practical sense for a belief to be rational.) Research now informs debate more efficiently, via a regular Update/Information Service to schools and parents.

Hypotheses are tried carefully, tested and reported on (via the improved information systems) and there is a far more sophisticated use of piloting of new ideas. As a consequence, proven practical ideas influence practice more speedily than in the past. This is helped greatly through the systematic and comprehensive involvement of class teachers in all aspects of research, development and monitoring of progress. The essential weakness of the educational debate of the 1990s was insufficient attention to what actually happens in classrooms, in ways in which demonstrably help teachers, parents and learners improve their practice. These days the debate is more open, less dominated by academics, administrators and politicians, and much more systematically focused on identifying and generalizing proven practical ideas. At the same time, there is more understanding of the need for stability and continuity, harmony and high morale.

More opportunities for teachers to engage in classroom research are now available. All teachers have the opportunity to use their classroom practice in researching and improving their own work in periods free of class-teaching duties. Higher degrees are linked more closely to practical situations. There are also closer links between researchers in other disciplines – health, management, industry, urban studies, media studies – as well as a growing internationalization in the research field, as common strands are identified.

One thing we have realized: 'good' often does not remain 'good' for long. Thus we plan for constant change. Paradoxically, we look for both stability and adaptability, we value the ability to sustain continuity and adjust to rapid change in ways which show an overriding sense of balance and judgement.

The different elements of the research field feed into the broad area of school effectiveness and school improvement. Since the 1990s, the considerable changes in our thinking about practice have modified our understanding of what good schools, at the moment, 'tend to do'. On the other hand, some of the general principles outlined in research in the 1970s and 1980s have proved reliable. The role of head teachers is clearly crucial, and a great deal of attention is now paid to their recruitment and to their personal and management support. All are given sabbatical leave after their first five years in post to enable them to take time out to visit other schools, engage in a critical study of their own school, support other heads and undergo a detailed, informal support interview to analyse progress.

It is increasingly common for head teachers to return to the classroom. In any case, all are expected to have a profound and practical understanding of the teaching/learning process, and to search constantly for ways to enhance this process in the school and community.

Business management of schools is now much more sophisticated: all schools have non-teaching finance managers, releasing head teachers from routine, administrative chores to act as strategic thinkers and team leaders, to move the educational aspects of the school forward. Small schools now team up into groups, for management and curriculum purposes. There are also much closer links between secondary and feeder primary schools – and schools commonly use satellite facilities, available for use by people of all age groups.

Leadership of these complex, open organizations is less hierarchical and more dedicated to creating access for teachers and the community and a lively, disciplined climate which draws in the support of children and parents at every stage. It is committed to making every possible use of available talent and enterprise. It is committed, above all, to developing the thinking and personal qualities of teachers and pupils as a *first principle*, from which all others flow.

Conclusion

In conclusion, the essential difference between the school of the 1990s and of the twenty-first century is our emphatic determination to adjust organizational procedures within the institution to suit the needs of individuals. Both primary and secondary schools in the 1990s were constrained by traditional practices and the diktat of timetables. We have learned to overcome such artificial constraints in the service of delivering a curriculum and teaching support appropriate to the needs and aspirations of all children. The whole apparatus is now geared to confidence building and achievement. Children no longer leave our schools thinking they have failed: we are achievement- rather than (old-style) examination-orientated. Parents and, significantly, children themselves are involved closely in the teaching/learning process. They learn *how* and *why* and *in what way* they are achieving and why educational endeavour is so important to them and to others.

Paradoxically in all this there is both more variety and more consensus. There is consensus on principles and a more cogently understood sense of what quality learning is about; but there is also a much greater emphasis on initiative and variety of response at school level (we now understand, for instance, how some children at some points in their learning career require more containment and discipline and others more freedom and more access to play). There is an interchange between schools, more involvement with further and higher education at local level, and schools are open from 7.30 a.m. to 9.00 p.m. and at weekends, for children and parents to use as they wish. Schools are, on the whole, more exciting places to be than in the past, and teaching is certainly a more rewarding profession.

Conclusion

Primary education has recently become a political battleground and has suffered accordingly. It would be easy to dwell on the stress felt by beleaguered head teachers, and the demoralization of the teaching profession as more and more control is taken by the central government. But this political attention is not all negative. The 'politics' of primary education goes beyond the party politics or the impact of dogma on the governing of schools. As the chapters in this book make clear, the real debate, like the evidence that supports it, is at a deeper level. How can children best learn and how can teachers best help them?

There is always bound to be some tension, even antipathy, between the needs of children and government reforms. It is a rare event when both coincide. For it seems there is bound to be a perpetual difference between the potential and the reality, between what children could achieve and what they do. This might seem bleak, but it is only by looking at the opportunities missed, by facing up to the possibilities unfulfilled, that the potential of children can be properly realized.

There are two distinct strands of feeling in this book. One is of concern. This is for the teachers and their pupils in a time of fear and uncertainty. One can pick on phrases like 'reign of terror' and 'demoralization', and sympathize with the teachers who seem to get little real support for all their efforts, and with the pupils who are all clearly not fulfilling their great potential at the most crucial time of their lives. Beyond the propaganda about 'rising' or 'falling' standards lies the evidence about what is actually happening in schools, and this is disturbing.

But the core feeling in this book is not bleak. In all the chapters there is also a sense of hope and optimism. The scrutiny afforded to primary education might show the difficulties and the failures of policy, but it also reveals what could and should be done. By giving a voice to the needs of children as well as their abilities, and by being willing to act on the evidence, primary schools could go through a period of renewal and transformation. Bill Percival always blended the realistic with the optimistic. The chapters in this book do the same.

Teachers in primary schools need all the help they can get. One day, perhaps in the new millennium, society as a whole will take its education system seriously and look at it not as a political shuttlecock but as a means to securing a sound future.

Index

ROLES AND RESPONSIBILITIES IN THE PRIMARY SCHOOL
CHANGING DEMANDS, CHANGING PRACTICES

Rosemary Webb and Graham Vulliamy

- How are teachers planning and implementing the National Curriculum at Key Stage 2?
- How have the recent policy and legislative changes affected the roles and responsibilities of class teachers, curriculum coordinators, deputy headteachers and headteachers?
- How are primary schools managing the current plethora of innovations and what can be learned from their experience?

Based on qualitative research in 50 schools throughout England and Wales, this book portrays teachers' work as it is currently experienced in the post-ERA context of multiple innovations. It examines the impact of the National Curriculum and assessment on classroom practice, curriculum organization and planning at Key Stage 2. Drawing on the wealth of ideas and successful practices shared with the authors by the teachers in the study, it demonstrates how classteachers, curriculum coordinators, deputy headteachers and headteachers are tackling the new demands of their expanding roles. An analysis of the management of change reveals a growing tension between collegial and top-down directive managerial styles, which is fundamentally affecting the culture of primary schools. Through presenting what is actually happening in primary schools in contrast to prescribed educational orthodoxies, this book makes a vital contribution to the debate on the future of primary education.

Contents
Introduction and methodology – The changing context of primary education – Changing demands on classroom practice – Changing curriculum organization and planning – The changing role of the curriculum coordinator – The changing role of the deputy headteacher – The changing role of the headteacher – Managing whole school change in the post-ERA primary school – References – Index.

192pp   0 335 19472 9 (Paperback)   0 335 19473 7 (Hardback)

MENTORING AND DEVELOPING PRACTICE IN PRIMARY SCHOOLS
SUPPORTING STUDENT TEACHER LEARNING IN SCHOOLS

Anne Edwards and Jill Collison

Is school-based initial teacher training just another burden to be imposed on primary school teachers or is it an exciting new development which could be the key to the development of primary education?

This book will be of interest to anyone who wants student teachers to make the most of their time in primary schools. Its central theme is that students learn best when supported by *active mentors*. Active mentors are learning teachers who are able to develop as professionals in the schools in which they work. These schools may in turn have much to gain from closer relationships with higher education. Throughout the book primary education is described as a community of practice to which all primary education specialists, wherever they are based, have contributions to make. The book is designed as a key text for modular staff development programmes in either schools or universities. Evidence from classroom mentoring is provided as starting points for the development of mentor practices through action research. In addition each chapter is followed by suggestions for further reading and most end with ideas for professional development activities for mentors and their students.

The text pulls no punches on how demanding mentoring is but provides a wealth of advice on the development of students, mentors and ultimately of schools. It will be invaluable reading for mentors in schools and tutors in higher education institutions.

Contents
Section 1 – Frameworks and themes – Students as learners – Section 2 – Mentoring conversations – Mentoring in action in classrooms – Running seminars – Mentoring and subject knowledge – Pedagogy and initial teacher training – Mentoring and assessing – Section 3 – Mentors as researchers – Mentoring and school development – Making the most of relationships with higher education – Endpiece – References – Index.

192pp   0 335 19565 2 (Paperback)   0 335 19566 0 (Hardback)